THE POWER WITHIN

BECOME
BULLY-PROOF

STRATEGIES THAT EMPOWER VICTIMS TO
BECOME BULLY-PROOF

Ian Findley

First published by Busybird Publishing 2025

Copyright © 2025 Ian Findley

ISBN:
Paperback: 978-1-923501-11-9
Ebook: 978-1-923501-12-6

This work is copyright. Apart from any use permitted under the *Copyright Act 1968*, no part of this publication may be reproduced, stored in a retrieval system or transmitted in any form or by any means, electronic, mechanical, photocopying, recording or otherwise, without the prior written permission of Ian Findley.

The information in this book is based on the author's experiences and opinions. The author and publisher disclaim responsibility for any adverse consequences that may result from use of the information contained herein. Permission to use any external content has been sought by the author. Any breaches will be rectified in further editions of the book.

Cover Image: Ian Findley

Cover design: Ian Findley

Layout and typesetting: Busybird Publishing

Busybird Publishing
2/118 Para Road
Montmorency, Victoria
Australia 3094
www.busybird.com.au

Contents

ABOUT THE AUTHOR		1
INTRODUCTION		3
1	UNHEALED WOUNDS Is bullying taking a toll on you or someone you care about? "Bullying has more victims than just the initial target"	5
2	THE POWER PLAY Where is your power? "If you can't hurt me, you can't bully me"	10
3	WORKING TOGETHER Being involved in your recovery "Empowerment – The need for a team effort"	12
4	FACE YOUR FEAR, FIND YOUR STRENGTH: Strategies - What changes do you want to see? "The change was remarkable"	26
5	TAKE CHARGE The Path to Emotional Freedom - Self-control "Empowering – Self-control – Power of positive thinking"	32
6	STANDING STRONG The Power of Body Language "If you look strong, you will begin to feel strong"	42
7	MASTERING SOCIAL SKILLS Building Bridges "Building on a Solid Foundation"	49
8	TURN FEAR INTO STRENGTH How do I build Confidence? "Above all else, do not show your fear"	58
9	HUMOUR AS ARMOUR Building Resilience in the Face of Bullying	64

10	THE POWER OF IGNORING: FROM ACTING TO REALITY Acting Strong: Using Drama to build resilience against bullying "Drama - the Art of Pretending"	73
11	ONLINE BULLYING What can I do about Cyberbullying? "The Path to Cyber Resilience"	81
12	THE ROAD TO RESILIENCE How can I stand up and be strong? "Developing Assertiveness & Resilience"	87
13	RESTORING HOPE Responding to Bullying in Schools To The Parents: "Embracing Restorative Approaches in Dealing with Bullying"	98
14	FAMILY SUPPORT Supporting your child through Bullying. "Be wise and careful in the advice you give your children"	110
CONCLUSION		117

ABOUT THE AUTHOR

Ian has dedicated over 40 years to supporting and caring for young people, families and educators within school communities. His career spans roles as a teacher, year-level coordinator and school chaplain/counsellor, bringing him face-to-face with the unique challenges today's young people encounter. Throughout these years, Ian has focused especially on bullying - a subject that has profoundly influenced his approach to education, counselling and pastoral care.

Ian is the author of four books and a dedicated family man, with four grown children and nine grandchildren. His personal life has only strengthened his commitment to nurturing resilience, empathy and even a sense of fun in young people.

Academically, Ian earned a Bachelor of Arts with majors in Music and Religious Studies from La Trobe University. Driven to support others, he later completed a Diploma in Counselling and a Certificate in Supervision. In addition to his experience as a counsellor, he is a trained, qualified mediator.

As a school chaplain, Ian became a trusted figure for countless students, families and staff members, offering pastoral care, counselling and compassionate guidance. An accomplished storyteller, he uses real-life narratives to convey powerful lessons and insights in his books. Through these stories, Ian combines practical strategies with empathy, encouraging resilience and empowerment for those being bullied and strategies and support material to the people who are supporting them.

        Website: www.ifindbooks.com.au

        Email: ifindbooks3@gmail.com

INTRODUCTION

Are You Being Bullied?

Are you a parent concerned about your child being bullied?

Are you a teacher, counsellor, chaplain, social worker or youth worker supporting someone affected by bullying?

If you answered yes to any of these questions, **then this book is for you**.

The Power Within is crafted to support and uplift individuals suffering due to bullying. The primary aim of this book is to speak directly to those who have experienced bullying, empowering them with practical strategies and tools to not only survive but thrive. However, this book also serves as a valuable resource for families and professionals—teachers, counsellors, chaplains, youth workers, welfare workers and parents—who are dedicated to assisting individuals in their journey to recovery.

A Dual-Purpose Approach

While the content is written in a manner that speaks directly to the bullied individual, it is equally beneficial for those in supportive roles. The strategies and exercises provided can be utilised by parents, professionals and caregivers to guide and reinforce the healing process. This dual-purpose approach ensures that the material is accessible and practical for both personal use and as a supportive tool in various settings.

Practical Strategies with Guided Exercises

Each skill presented in this book is accompanied by corresponding exercises. These exercises are designed to allow individuals to practice and develop the necessary skills to overcome the impacts of bullying. By actively engaging with these exercises, readers can build resilience, confidence, and a sense of empowerment.

The techniques covered include:

- **Assertiveness**: Learning to stand firm and reclaim personal power
- **Body Language**: Communicating confidence non-verbally
- **Finding Inner Strength**: Tapping into existing resilience
- **Facing Fear**: Overcoming barriers that hinder progress
- **Using Humour and Deflection**: Reducing the impact of bullying through humour
- **Using drama**: Empowerment through acting
- **Building Social Skills**: Creating connections that bolster confidence
- **Resilience and Recovery**: Healing and growing stronger internally
- **Handling Cyberbullying**: Protecting oneself in the digital realm

These techniques are grounded in counselling practice, research, education and real-life experiences. They have proven effective in helping individuals overcome bullying and emerge stronger.

CHAPTER ONE

UNHEALED WOUNDS

Is bullying taking a toll on you or someone you care about?

"Bullying has more victims than just the initial target"

It's 9.20am on Monday, 26 February 1993. I'm in my office at my new school, planning the day's activities, when there's a knock at the door. I look up as a woman enters, someone I've never met before. Her eyes are heavy with emotion; she's clearly fighting to hold back tears. "Are you the new Chaplain?" she asks, voice strained. I invite her to sit. Barely managing to hold herself together, she begins to sob. Between her tears, she says "Why? Why did he do it? Why did he do this to me?"

Grace's teenage son Liam, had taken his own life. As she searches for answers, she tells me her story, replaying that night over and over in agonising detail. Two years ago, on a Friday night, Liam had come home from a run. He made himself a sandwich, left his usual mess on the kitchen bench and went to his room. That was the last time she saw him alive. When she found him, Liam lay motionless in his room, he had taken his own life.

As Grace seeks to understand why, her pain sharpens. The more we uncover, the clearer it becomes that Liam had endured bullying - humiliating, cruel and isolating. He had been alone in his suffering for nearly two years. The burden of her unanswered questions deepens her sorrow and guilt. *"Why didn't he tell me? I'm his mother. I could have helped him."*

Liam's experience was not unique. The impact of bullying goes beyond the initial target. Studies reveal that even bystanders, families and communities feel the aftershocks of such trauma. Every year, bullying leaves lasting scars on countless lives. As I learned more, I realised that some people who had faced bullying turned their pain inward, while others unleashed it outward, impacting those around them. I recalled an article from Sydney, detailing the tragic story of a student who stood before his class, looked his peers in the eye and then shot himself in front of them. What was he trying to say? What impact would that act have on the people who witnessed it?

Moved deeply by Liam's story, I dedicated myself to understanding bullying and finding ways to combat it. The questions were clear, yet the answers felt elusive:

- What is bullying?
- Why do students bully?
- Why are some children targeted while others are not?
- How can we effectively help those who bully, to change?
- How can we effectively support people like Liam, who suffer in silence?

Through study, research, student and parent surveys, I uncovered the intensity of bullying's true impact. Parents, still haunted by their own school experiences from decades earlier, shared stories as fresh as if they'd happened yesterday. Some had even reframed their own children's experiences in light of these old wounds. For many, bullying remained an unresolved trauma - unhealed and persistent.

In my role as a school Chaplain, I often encountered students who showed signs of distress - social isolation, poor self-esteem, difficulty making friends, anger outbursts, depression. What's alarming is how often these struggles can be linked to bullying. Despite the seriousness of the problem, we as a society have failed to adequately address it.

It is time to revisit the original question, to look closely and honestly at the environments where bullying thrives. No longer can we dismiss bullying as a "normal" part of growing up. The suffering, silence and despair of people like Liam demand that we take a stand.

One day I was called out of a meeting at school to speak with a parent who had informed the office staff that I was needed urgently. This mother had driven nearly all the way to her place of employment that morning, but because she was concerned for the safety and wellbeing of her daughter, she felt the need to turn around and come directly to the school. Her daughter was going through some difficult experiences within her peer group, a situation that I was aware of. The girl's mother was distressed and worried that her daughter was being bullied and might be unable to cope. As this mother spoke her emotional state heightened.

> *"I was bullied at school and I don't want my daughter to go through what I went through".*

Her daughter was not being bullied at all. There was definitely conflict between peers but her daughter displayed all the social skills and confidence that kept her safe from becoming a victim. Unfortunately, this mother's own demons were being resurrected. What she believed may be happening to her daughter had re-opened old wounds that were hidden deep within herself. This mother was reliving the emotion, the fears and pain that had caused her so much trauma when she was at school many years ago. This mother was still a victim.

As a part of my research, I undertook some surveys with students and parents. The purpose of these surveys was to create an avenue where I could obtain information as to what people thought, felt and what was really happening in our schools. If people could speak anonymously without fear of retribution, they might be more willing to speak up and assist. The response from parents in particular was very moving.

The stories they told of their children, as well as their own personal experiences from 15-20 years ago, flowed forward as if they were experiencing them today. I occasionally thought that I could see the stains of their tears on the paper. Many of these stories moved me greatly.

As a school Chaplain, I found myself working more and more with students who were:

- experiencing social isolation
- displaying signs of poor self-esteem
- refusing to attend school
- having regular outbursts of anger
- displaying behavioural concerns
- experiencing difficulties in making and keeping friends
- unhappy or depressed.

To my surprise, I discovered that many of these students were suffering as a result of bullying.

Bullying is a serious problem. We can no longer stand back and dismiss the issue lightly. The impact of bullying can be severe and the original questions society has failed to address adequately need to be revisited.

- What can we teach young people to help minimise the impact of bullying?
- Can they learn how to be safe?
- Can they learn the secrets to personal empowerment?
- Can they learn how to protect their power?
- Can people learn to be bullyproof?

I believe they can. With the right knowledge and support, young people can stand strong, resisting and overcoming attempts to bully them.

CHAPTER TWO

THE POWER PLAY

Where is your power?

"If you can't hurt me, you can't bully me"

"I'm going to bully you today" said a colleague of mine, jokingly standing in an aggressive manner.
　"No, you're not."
　"Yes I am."
　"No, you're not."
　"Just watch me."
　"You can't bully me."
　"Why can't I?"
　"Because bullying is about power and you don't have any power over me, so give it your best shot."
　I stood strongly with my head up looking him firmly in the eye.
　"Well, I'll just have to find someone else to bully then," he said as he backed down and walked away.

This light-hearted banter can offer valuable insights into understanding bullying. To make real progress in addressing bullying, it's essential to recognise what bullying truly is. At its core, bullying is about power - specifically, the abuse of power. People who struggle to maintain or protect their sense of power often become victims. Teaching people how to use their power responsibly and how to safeguard it when faced with challenges can make a significant difference. The ability to respond assertively or to deflect bullying behaviours plays a critical role in determining whether a person becomes a victim or stands resilient against it.

Most people would list the following behaviours as bullying:
- Name calling
- Pushing
- Making fun of others
- Making threats
- Rude comments
- Making comments about a person's appearance
- Mimicking
- Punching
- Interfering with another's property, and so on.

Most would agree that these behaviours can be hurtful and potentially damaging. But it's important to recognise that, in different circumstances, these same behaviours can be positive, friendly and even relationship-building. Many of us engage in this type of playful banter with our friends every day. The ability to laugh and have fun together is crucial. When a friend does or says something silly, we point it out, enjoy a laugh and perhaps tease them a little - it's all in good fun. Interestingly, I tend not to joke with those I don't know well or don't particularly like, because these light-hearted exchanges are rooted in trust and comfort. Take, for example, the "threats" made against me by a colleague. Far from being negative, they actually brought us closer together. These exchanges were a way of saying, "I enjoy your company, I accept you and you're fun to be around." From hiding each other's coffee cups to playfully pointing out each other's awkward moments, these are behaviours we engage in for fun.

So, when are these actions bullying, and when are they not?

It's simple: when the behaviours are hurtful and damaging, it is 'bullying'.

CHAPTER THREE

WORKING TOGETHER

Being involved in your recovery

"Empowerment – the need for support"

In the following chapters, I will share fundamental strategies that have proven to be effective in helping people overcome the impact of bullying and start to rebuild their confidence.

Parent statement:

"I was worried that without help she would find it difficult to reconnect with her peers and cope with future feelings of rejection or criticism."

Are You Carrying Emotional Wounds from Bullying?

Bullying can leave deep emotional scars that aren't always visible. Recognising these wounds is a vital step toward healing.

You might be experiencing such wounds if you:

- Feel powerless or believe you have little control over your life

- Struggle with low self-esteem and diminished confidence

- Experience heightened anxiety, find making eye contact difficult or social interactions challenging

- Speak softly or hesitate to express yourself
- Withdraw from others, avoiding social situations
- Feel isolated, rejected or disconnected from those around you

Expecting someone who has endured severe bullying to re-enter the environment in which the bullying has occurred and function well without new skills and support is unrealistic and potentially harmful. Placing a "wounded person" back into a community without equipping them with skills, coping strategies and a support system may leave them vulnerable. Without these essential resources, they could once again become easy targets for bullies, putting them at risk for further emotional and psychological harm.

Bullying can significantly diminish your sense of power, confidence and self-esteem. In the coming chapters, I will share fundamental strategies that have proven effective in helping people overcome the impact of bullying, building resilience and a sense of safety. These techniques are proven, straightforward yet powerful, and anyone with basic people skills can put them into practice successfully. My focus of support centres on **empowerment**. Every suggestion and activity included here is designed to heal, equip and strengthen, to help people not only rise above bullying but also to cope with life's challenges in healthy, constructive ways.

Each person is unique, possessing their own set of skills, interests, and personality traits. Consequently, experiences with bullying and the subsequent support required can vary significantly. Factors such as the nature and severity of the bullying, individual resilience, and current life circumstances all influence how someone is affected. While some individuals may exhibit visible signs of distress, others might internalise their experiences, making it challenging to recognise their need for support. It's essential to understand that there's no universal reaction to bullying. Acknowledging and respecting these individual differences is crucial in providing effective assistance and fostering healing.

Healing from bullying begins with a crucial shift: recognising that while you are not to blame for what happened, you have the power to shape your recovery. This journey is about reclaiming your power, sense of self, rebuilding your confidence, finding and releasing the power within.

We will approach this process with great sensitivity. It's important to understand that you are not responsible for what has happened to you and you don't have to face this alone. However, your active participation is vital. Engaging in your healing empowers you to make decisions that foster growth and resilience.

By taking ownership of your recovery, you begin to restore self-belief and confidence. This doesn't mean solving everything on your own, but rather collaborating with trusted individuals—be it family, counsellors or supportive peers—to navigate the path forward.

Remember, the impact of bullying can lead to feelings of shame, self-doubt and isolation. Acknowledging these feelings is a step towards healing. You're not alone, and with the right support and mindset, you can overcome these challenges and emerge stronger.

Our Starting Points

- **Affirming Courage:** Acknowledging your bravery in facing this challenge head-on

- **Encouraging Positive Risks:** Supporting your willingness to take small, constructive steps and try new approaches

- **Fostering Commitment:** Finding the motivation to see the healing process through

- **Empowering Ownership:** Reassuring yourself that this is your journey and you are in control. I'm here to guide and support you every step of the way

Discovering Positive Spaces

Think about the places and activities where you feel different from how you do when you're being bullied. These environments can offer valuable insights and opportunities for positive change. For example, someone who feels lonely and isolated at school might feel happy, safe and accepted at their swimming club. Many people reveal different sides of themselves in settings like scouts, youth groups, sports teams, dance classes or other clubs where they feel relaxed and valued. Recognising these positive spaces can help you understand your strengths and build confidence. Engaging more in such activities can be a step towards healing and personal growth. In reflection I recognised that I was a different person at my youth group to who I was at school. I was shy, quiet, timid, lacking in confidence and afraid at school. However, I was outgoing, confident, loud and popular at my youth group. These are important things to recognise. If you have the skills in one setting, you can learn how to transfer them to another.

If you discover that you feel more at ease in these other environments, consider exploring the following questions:

Replace "Scouts" with your own activity.

- What feels different for you when you're at Scouts compared to when you're at school?
- Why do you think being at Scouts feels different for you?
- How do you act at Scouts compared to how you act at school?
- Do you like the person you are when you're at Scouts?
- How does being at Scouts make you feel, compared to being at school?
- Do you notice a connection between how you act and how you feel in these different places?

- How do people treat you at Scouts?

- Do you find yourself treating others differently when you're at Scouts?

- Why do you think people treat you differently at Scouts than they do at school?

- What do you think makes it possible for you to feel happy and included at Scouts but not at school?

- How might we be able to bring some of these positive skills or experiences into school life?

If you can demonstrate certain skills in one setting, it's simply a matter of building your confidence to transfer those skills and apply them in a different environment, such as school. To put it more strongly: if you can do it in one setting, you can learn to do it in another. The skills are already present; they simply need to be transferred and applied in a different context. It's about recognising your strengths and helping you see and accept that you have the capability to use those same strengths in other areas of your life. I encourage and hope to support you as you begin to grow more confident in bringing these abilities into school, creating a more positive and empowering experience for yourself.

Determine your strengths. This approach can reveal the innate skills you have. You can harness these strengths and build on them to aid your recovery and overcome the impacts of bullying.

Confidence and power are closely associated with an individual's sense of acceptance. When someone feels comfortable and accepted, it can significantly enhance their confidence and sense of authority. Both acceptance and confidence are often connected to an individual's skills and achievements.

Explore:
- What are the things you're good at?
- What do you enjoy doing the most?
- How do you feel when you do things well?
- How does it affect your confidence?
- What happens to those feelings of confidence when you're at school and facing bullying?
- How might you learn to stand strong and protect your sense of power, even when things feel difficult?

Recognising Your Strengths Through Relationships

Think about the safe people you interact with—friends, family, teachers, neighbours—and how you feel in those relationships. Identifying situations where you feel confident and in control can highlight your personal strengths.

Once you've recognised these moments, consider how the skills and qualities you demonstrate in these relationships can help you cope with and overcome bullying. These strengths can serve as valuable resources in building resilience and confidence.

Questions to Guide Your Reflection:
- What are your relationships like with your friends, brothers and/or sisters?
- In these relationships, do you feel a sense of power, influence or control?
- How do you respond if one of these people called you a name or did something you didn't like?
- How do you feel if one of these people called you a name or treated you in a way you didn't like?

- Are these feelings different from how you feel when you're being bullied at school?

- How might you bring the confidence and strength from these relationships into your experience at school?

These points are not exhaustive. It's important to recognise that we cannot predict all the answers or expand the process too far without becoming overwhelmed. Work with the information discovered, start setting some simple achievable goals and focus on building your confidence while learning new skills as you go. It is always good to work with and talk with another person about what you are trying to achieve and understand. Your parents, a counsellor, a youth worker, a school Chaplain or a trusted friend can assist you with feedback and even assist in roleplays.

If you're facing bullying and feel uncertain about seeking help, it's important to know that support is available and reaching out is a proactive step toward empowerment.

Seeking Support:
Begin by confiding in someone you trust—this could be a parent, teacher, school counsellor, youth worker, or chaplain. Many schools offer specialised programs aimed at building resilience and addressing bullying. For instance, the FRIENDS programs are Australian-developed, cognitive behaviour therapy-based initiatives designed to build life-long resilience in individuals, families, schools and communities. Additionally, the Friendly Schools initiative works with families to improve understanding and self-efficacy to discuss bullying with their children.

If you're hesitant to seek support due to feelings of embarrassment or reluctance, consider bringing this book with you when you talk to a trusted adult. Sharing what you're working on can provide context and facilitate understanding. It's crucial to find someone who will support your goals without interfering or exacerbating the situation.

Taking Responsibility:

While it's natural to expect parents or schools to intervene, it's equally important for you to take an active role in addressing the situation. This doesn't mean facing it alone, but rather collaborating with trusted individuals to develop strategies that empower you and equip you for future occurrences. Remember, seeking support is not a sign of weakness but a step toward reclaiming your safety, confidence and wellbeing.

Clara was a shy, timid 14-year-old girl in Year 8, with limited social skills, low self-esteem and little confidence. She felt isolated and unwanted by a group of girls in her class who found fun in ridiculing and mocking her. Clara would sit silently with her head down as the girls mocked her, laughing and making derogatory comments about her work, her personality and her withdrawn nature. Over time, she became emotionally shattered, lonely and frightened. She spent much of her time in tears. Her parents, devastated and unsure of how to help, had no choice but to contact the school and demand action be taken against the girls involved.

I arranged for Clara's parents to bring her into school, as she had not been attending for over a week. It took a few days to get her to agree, but eventually the meeting was scheduled. I believed that meeting at school was crucial in helping Clara face and overcome her fears, though I was prepared to visit her at home if necessary. Clara's parents were as hurt and upset as she was. They were angry and determined, demanding, fighting to protect their daughter while desperately looking for a way to ease her pain. Clara, however, was responding in a different way. She was withdrawn, passive, fearful and unsure how to cope. Sitting quietly through the meeting, she stared at the floor. When she did speak, she barely whispered a few words. Most of the information I gathered about the impact of the bullying came from her parents.

"She just won't come to school anymore."
"She is scared, miserable, and won't stop crying."
"She spends most of her time in her room, lying on her bed, sobbing."

"She doesn't have any friends."
"She won't talk about it, and we don't know what to do."
"It's taken us this long to understand what's happening."

Her parents' efforts were not helping her much at all. They made it clear: "If the school can't fix this, we will." I wasn't sure what they meant by that, but fortunately we didn't have to find out because I explained to them the **Shared Responsibility** method the school used to address bullying and how successful it had been in the past.

The **Shared Responsibility** method is detailed in my first book, **Shared Responsibility: Beating Bullying in Australian Schools**. **Shared Responsibility** is a restorative program that supports the victims and empowers the bullies by getting them to reflect and understand the impact of their actions on others. It appeals to and builds on empathy. It involves the bullies and places them in a position to come up with a solution to solve the problem. It's amazing just how effective this has been. Where in the past, schools have dealt ineffectively with bully incidents by limiting their procedures to punishment and threats, **Shared Responsibility** has evidenced a much higher success rate in stopping the bullying and assisting the victims to be and feel safe.

At this point, Clara's parents were starting to calm down. They realised that the school's approach, while different from what they had expected, was likely a better way to help Clara feel safe and assist her in returning to school.

What they really wanted was simple: a happy daughter who would attend school, feel safe and be free from intimidation and ridicule.

We all agreed on these goals.

Clara was being supported and her parents could see that. They reluctantly agreed to allow the school to try the **Shared Responsibility** method, but not without a final threat: "If the school doesn't fix it, we will."

At this point, I needed to hear from Clara herself. I needed her permission to assist and for her to commit to being a part of the solution. She needed to share in the responsibility and be involved in the process. With a nervous whisper, she said, "I suppose it's all right." I made it clear that we wouldn't know if this approach would be successful unless she was willing to help us by returning to school. This would be her first step toward sharing the responsibility for solving her problem. Her parents quickly interrupted, saying, "Don't worry, we will get her there." But I needed to hear it from Clara.

Her parents decided to keep her home a few more days so the school could arrange and conduct the **Shared Responsibility** meeting before Clara returned. I recommended that Clara commit to ongoing support to help her recover and equip her for re-integration into the school community. Without it, I feared she would struggle to reconnect with her peers and cope with feelings of rejection or criticism. Her parents agreed that this would be helpful, but Clara, though silently reluctant, later communicated through her parents that she didn't need counselling and that everything would be fine once the bullying stopped. Despite her reluctance, I insisted she meet with me at least once so I could explain how the support would be beneficial. I also arranged for her to be met by a few students who were willing to assist her transition back into school comfortably.

When Clara returned to school, she nervously attended the appointment. Her body language was weak and her confidence was low. She listened without engaging or committing to anything. Later, through her parents, I learned that she had decided not to follow through with the counselling. Over the next few weeks, I found it difficult to get information from Clara. I needed to know if the **Shared Responsibility** meeting had been successful, if she was okay, and if the bullying had stopped. Clara was reluctant to speak, so I reached out to her parents several times to confirm that the bullying had ceased. They were satisfied with the school's handling of the bullying but expressed concern about Clara's ongoing unhappiness and lack of self-worth. I took the opportunity to observe Clara and her peers in class and during break times. She quietly hovered on the edge of groups, not fully participating. The students who had helped her return to school were trying hard to include her, even fussing over her at times.

The **Shared Responsibility** meeting had been successful in stopping the bullying, but Clara's self-esteem, confidence and social skills had been so damaged that she continued to feel isolated and unhappy. She didn't know how to fit in, belong, or enjoy herself. She was suspicious of everyone and dependent on constant attention and inclusion. When others made an effort to include her, she was okay; when she felt overlooked, she was miserable. Eventually, Clara realised she needed more support and attended two counselling sessions. They were helpful, but not enough to fully address the deeper issues. Clara made some progress in confidence and learned some basic social skills, but unfortunately, she didn't take full responsibility for seeing the process through.

Clara's story illustrates the importance of people sharing responsibility in solving the problem of bullying. As I mentioned earlier, it is not enough for a person to simply expect the school or their parents to stop the bullying without taking any personal responsibility for preventing it from happening again. Without this learning, the situation is likely to re-occur. Clara, despite the school's intervention, still struggled with self-esteem and confidence. She relied heavily on external support but did not fully embrace her role in the process.

I cannot overstate the importance of the person being actively involved in the process and sharing responsibility for achieving a positive outcome, even if it's in the smallest of ways. When a person is not engaged in the process, they can feel even more weak and helpless than they did before. The act of participating - whether in decision-making or completing small tasks - gradually builds confidence and their sense of control. Every step forward, no matter how small, contributes to the person's personal growth and healing. By giving them a role in their own recovery, we help them reclaim their power and develop the resilience needed to navigate life's challenges. It's not just about stopping the bullying; it's about supporting and empowering the person to feel safe, capable, valued and in control of their life.

Practice Exercise 1: "Small Steps Make Me Stronger"

Purpose:
To help you to start taking small but meaningful steps toward building your confidence, social skills, and a sense of personal responsibility.

What you'll need:
- A notebook or journal
- A quiet space
- 10–15 minutes a day

PART 1: *Noticing My Feelings*

Exercise
Each day for one week, take a few minutes to write down your answers to the following questions:

1. **How am I feeling today?**
   - (Try to be specific: sad, angry, anxious, lonely, okay, hopeful...)

2. **What made me feel that way?**
   - (A person? A thought? A situation?)

3. **What did I do about it?**
   - (Did I talk to someone? Did I hide? Did I ignore it?)

Goal: Start recognising your emotional patterns and responses, just like Clara needed to do. You can't change what you're not aware of.

PART 2: *My Brave Act*
Each day, choose one small action that shows you are part of the solution. Pick from the list or write your own:

- Make eye contact with someone and smile
- Say hello to a classmate or teacher
- Join a group conversation, even if just to listen
- Ask someone a question about their day
- Speak to a trusted adult about how you're feeling
- Attend a meeting or counselling session, even if you don't feel like talking.

Write down:
- What did I do today that took a little courage?
- How did it feel afterwards?
- What might I try tomorrow?

Goal: To practice showing up and participating in your own healing, even in small ways.

PART 3: *Responsibility Reflection*

Once a week, reflect on this:

- What have I done to help make things better for myself this week?
- What have others done to help me?
- What can I do next week to keep moving forward?

Optional: Share your reflections with someone you trust.

Why This Matters

Just like Clara, you might feel like everything depends on others stepping in to help. And yes—getting help is important. But your **real strength grows** when *you* take part, even in small ways.

When you make decisions, take small brave steps, and share honestly, you're not just surviving bullying—you're building your **resilience**, confidence and future happiness.

CHAPTER FOUR

FACE YOUR FEAR – FIND YOUR STRENGTH

Strategies - What changes do you want to see?

"The change was remarkable"

"I had only been in my new secondary school two days before I was pushed, kicked, insulted and had my books thrown on the ground."

After just two days in her new school, Mahdi found herself being tormented by a boy in her class whom she'd never met before. She'd experienced some bullying in primary school, but nothing like this. Mahdi was assigned a locker above Ben's and, without warning, she was repeatedly shoved aside as Ben claimed the space he believed was rightfully his.

Mahdi tried to hold her ground, only to be met with a stream of rude names and comments about her appearance, all in front of her new peers. Other students responded in ways that encouraged Ben, fuelling his hurtful and aggressive behaviour by laughing at him. Ben was clearly trying to establish himself as the "tough" guy, striving to be funny, cool and in control.

For Mahdi, this marked the beginning of an unrelenting and targeted assault. Within days, her confidence plummeted and she dreaded going to her locker. Even in class, Ben's loud, aggressive presence made her feel trapped.

At home, Mahdi broke down, crying uncontrollably as she explained the situation to her parents. She didn't want to return to school, but her father encouraged her to be strong, urging her not to let one boy get to her. She clung to her parents' advice: "If it continues, tell the teacher."

Sure enough, Ben picked up where he'd left off. Overwhelmed and unsure of what else to do, Mahdi tearfully confided in her home group teacher. Her teacher, following the school's anti-bullying protocol, documented the incident and escalated it to the coordinator and was passed on to me. Together, we set the process in motion. Mahdi was commended for her courage to speak up and she shared her story. She was open about her feelings of fear, hurt, humiliation, embarrassment and her desperate wish for the bullying to end. I explained the **Shared Responsibility** method for addressing bullying in our school.

Mahdi set a goal; she just wanted the bullying to stop. It wasn't long before she felt comfortable and gave us permission to proceed.

However, Mahdi voiced some concern about returning to class:

What would her classmates think of her?

What would she say if they asked where she had been?

What if Ben or others pick on her even more for "dobbing?

What if she couldn't handle it and broke down in tears again?

In preparing Mahdi for her return to class, I emphasised the importance of projecting energy and a positive body language. We discussed how her classmates might react if she entered the room with her head down, moving slowly, looking hurt and upset. Mahdi could see that this approach would not be beneficial.

To help her regain confidence, we talked about the power of strong body language and how projecting a positive presence, even if she didn't feel that way, could influence her feelings and others' reactions. We practiced ways to enter class with her head held high, standing tall and using her natural, cheerful personality to convey confidence. I also helped her prepare brief, casual responses to anticipated questions, encouraging her to keep her tone steady and responses simple. She needed to display energy, appear happy and in control.

I informed Mahdi that Ben would soon be called to the office. Though still nervous, Mahdi agreed to do her part in creating a safer environment for herself. Mahdi left my office and returned to class with a clear plan, a renewed sense of confidence and far more energy than she'd displayed when she arrived.

The next day, Mahdi shared her experience with me:

"When I walked back to class, I had butterflies in my stomach. I didn't want to go, but I knew I had to. So, I took a few deep breaths, lifted my head and just went for it. The classroom door was locked, so I knocked and joked with the kids inside, asking them to let me in. They were expecting me to be upset, but I wasn't. I asked what they were working on and what I needed to catch up on. Mr. Findley had prepared me well.

Some kids asked, 'Are you alright?' and 'Where have you been?' I simply replied, 'I had to go to the office, no big deal.' I was surprised at how natural and confident I sounded. I felt like my old self again. I love to laugh and talk and soon I wasn't just pretending to be happy - I was happy. Ben didn't say anything. I think he was surprised to see me acting happy and energised. Shortly after, a note came from the office and Ben was called out. I just continued with class as normal."

Ben returned to class about thirty minutes later, he was noticeably quieter and didn't approach Mahdi or cause any trouble. The following day, Mahdi reported an even more remarkable shift. Not only had Ben stopped bullying her, but he was being polite, even standing back to give her first use of the lockers.

Mahdi's classmates took notice, asking, "What is it with Ben?"

Overnight, Ben's attitude had changed. Mahdi returned to school the next day happier and more self-assured than she'd been since starting secondary school.

Toward the end of the day, I checked in with Mahdi. She told me that Ben was being nice and had even asked her about her work on the computer, showing kindness she never expected.

The transformation was remarkable, with both Mahdi and Ben gaining something valuable from the experience. Mahdi emerged feeling happier, safer, more secure and visibly more confident. Through instruction, role-playing, risk-taking and empowerment, Mahdi had taken an active role in addressing the problems she was facing. The school and both young people shared the responsibility in solving the problem.

Ben responded positively to the Shared Responsibility Method. By involving both students in finding a solution, each gained insights that strengthened their empathy and respect for others, skills they could carry forward into their futures.

Practice Exercise 2: Walking Tall—Look Strong

Purpose:
To help you *prepare emotionally and physically* when re-entering difficult environments after experiencing bullying. This exercise focuses on posture, body language, emotional preparation and simple, confident communication.

Step 1: Visualise Success
Find a quiet place. Close your eyes and imagine yourself walking into a space where you've felt vulnerable. See yourself:

- Standing tall
- Head held high
- Big shoulders
- Breathing normally and calmly
- Smiling naturally
- Making appropriate eye contact with safe people.

Now imagine people looking at yourself, not with pity or judgment, but with curiosity or even respect because of how confident you seem. You feel strong, calm, and ready.

Repeat to yourself:

> *"I've got this. I belong here. I don't need to be afraid."*

Step 2: Practice Body Language
Stand up and practice the following:

- Walk across the room with confidence
- Keep your back straight, big shoulders, arms relaxed, breathing deeply but normally
- Smile naturally (even if it feels awkward)
- Practice entering a room walking with positive energy.

Optional: Use a mirror to check your posture. You can even record yourself on your phone and review how you come across.

Step 3: Prepare Calm, Casual Replies
Practice these short responses in a steady, neutral tone. Say them out loud:

- "I had to go to the office. All good now."
- "Just catching up on some stuff, no big deal."
- "Yeah, I'm okay. Thanks for asking."

Now try creating your own:
What's something *simple and calm* you could say if someone asked where you'd been or if you were okay?

Step 4: The Confidence Boost Checklist

Before re-entering a challenging space, check these off:

- ✓ I've practiced my posture and breathing
- ✓ I know what I'll say if someone asks questions
- ✓ I'm focusing on what *I* can control
- ✓ I remember that showing energy can help me feel better
- ✓ I've visualised myself walking in strong and calm

Reflection:

- How did this exercise make you feel?
- What part was the most helpful or surprising?
- Is there a friend or adult you can practice this with?

CHAPTER FIVE

TAKE CHARGE

The Path to Emotional Freedom

> *"The power of positive thinking"*
> *"Empowering"- Self-Control"*

What control do you have?

What degree of control do you want?

When responding to bullying, it's important to recognise that you cannot control others' actions or words. While you may sometimes influence their behaviour, true control lies only in our own thoughts, attitudes, responses, choices and actions.

Bullying often involves surrendering control over these personal aspects to the bully, which can lead to frustration, anxiety, fear, depression, anger and deep unhappiness. While you may not be able to change the bully's actions, you can learn to take charge of your own responses. Our goal is to own our sense of power and learn how to protect it.

For some, this process comes naturally, especially those who have never experienced bullying. But for others, it requires learning the skills to feel safe, secure and being in control ourselves.

In an ideal environment, bullies wouldn't exist. But in reality, they are unfortunately, part of our world. The solution does not solely lie in changing the bully's behaviour; it also lies in empowering the individual affected.

Should anyone else have control over how you feel or dictate what you do or don't do? One often overlooked impact of bullying is the experience of losing control over your own life. Research confirms that loss of control is a major contributor to conditions like anxiety, low self-esteem, uncontrolled anger, frustration, helplessness, fear, low self-confidence, lack of energy, powerlessness and even depression.

When we feel trapped in a position with no or little control, it can be overwhelming and negative emotions often arise. Some of these emotions come from when we attempt to control others - something ultimately beyond our abilities. Others arise when we lose control in areas where we should feel empowered, as happens when we become the target of bullying.

There is little value in stressing or worrying about things beyond our control. If something is out of our ability to control, it's best to accept it – move on and don't let it consume us with worry or stress. It is what it is. Instead, focus on what we can control and learn how to control it effectively.

When it comes to bullying, it's important to understand that others can only have control over our feelings if we allow it. While this truth may sound blunt, it forms a foundation for resilience and healing. By reclaiming our emotional autonomy, we take back our power. Adopting the mindset *"I will not allow others to control how I feel!"* is a crucial step toward breaking free from the hold that bullying can have. Building this foundation empowers those impacted to respond from a place of strength rather than vulnerability.

While we cannot control the bully, we can learn to control our reactions to them. Ultimately, isn't the common goal of life to find happiness, safety and peace within ourselves? Bullies often get inside our heads, robbing us of this inner peace and sense of joy. What I am saying is, no one and nothing should have the power to do that. Our happiness and peace are ours to guard - they're within our control. This is a foundational mindset and a powerful step toward reclaiming the stability and happiness we all deserve.

Let's take a moment to explore what happens in our minds when someone upsets us. Often, we begin to replay what they said or did, thinking it over until it consumes our thoughts. Our minds start traveling down paths of anger, retaliation or hurt. The more we dwell on these thoughts, the stronger and more consuming the negative emotions become. A small incident can quickly grow into something major and deeply hurtful.

This cycle can have a powerful impact on our lives, affecting everything from our sleep and concentration to our relationships, study and overall wellbeing. In some cases, it even leads to rifts that tear families apart. When we allow someone's actions to take control over our mind in this way, our goal of happiness and inner peace slips further away.

Our challenge then, is to recognise when this pattern begins and choose to respond differently. By breaking the habit of dwelling on negativity, we can refocus on what truly matters to us: living a life centred on peace, happiness, and resilience. This awareness is a critical step in retaining control and protecting our emotional wellbeing from unnecessary turmoil.

Now, let's do a simple exercise together. Let's practice taking control of our thinking. Yes, we can control what we choose to focus on in our minds. Since our goal is happiness and peace, we consciously decide not to go down the path of anger, hurt or frustration. We don't take the bait. When the impulse arises, we tell ourselves, "Don't go there." We make a clear decision not to dwell on it, because we know where it will lead and the emotional toll it will take.

Use self-talk: "Don't go there!" With practice, discipline and effort, this approach becomes easier - and experience has provided evidence that it works.

What do we truly gain if we let hurt, anger and frustration take control? Likely, we end up with arguments, fights, tension and unhappiness. Our life becomes consumed by negativity and in the process, we may hurt others and damage or lose what is really important to us. Sure, there might be a fleeting moment of satisfaction from feeling that we didn't let them "get away with it" but that satisfaction rarely lasts.

Ask yourself: Is this really where I want to be? Is this the life I want to have? Is this how I want to feel? Or, would you prefer to be peaceful, in control, be happy and be emotionally stable?

Choose the path that aligns with your true goals. By redirecting your thoughts, you reclaim peace and happiness as your foundation. Practicing this kind of control is a powerful step toward a life free from unnecessary turmoil and filled with intentional, lasting happiness. Self-control and self-value are very important.

I've been there many times myself.

Imagine this: a friend makes an offensive comment, thinking it's funny. I start pondering all the things I'd like to say in response. Old hurts resurface, growing bigger with each passing thought. Who does he think he is? My anger builds, and soon I'm spiralling: I won't go to his get-together next week. In fact, I'll never speak to him again. I should email him and tell him exactly what I think. I start crafting the words in my mind, replaying them over and over. Suddenly, I've convinced myself he was never a good friend. I'm ready to unfriend and block him on social media. I am now in a very negative emotional state.

Now pause for a moment—where has this taken me? Where is my happiness, my peace? I've traded my life's goals in a moment of anger, letting a small hurt rob me of my peace. The more we let these thoughts build, the further we drift from the life we desire.

Redirecting this focus is key. By choosing not to dwell on hurt, we protect our inner peace and keep our minds focused on what truly matters. It's a powerful decision to remain anchored in self-control and remain calm, regardless of what anyone says or does.

Now, let's take control and do it differently. He makes an offensive comment, thinking it's funny. In that moment, I see exactly where my thoughts are going and I quickly interrupt them with self-talk: *"Don't go there."* I choose to take control of my thinking. I want to stay in a positive place, so that's where I decide to stay.

It's not about fairness - it's about me and the kind of life I want to live. It's about me taking control of me. I refuse to let this negativity spiral and grow bigger than it needs to. I've been down those negative paths before and I know where they lead. I choose not to go there.

By making this choice, I retain my power and protect my peace. I stay grounded in the life I'm living, one where my happiness and control is in my own hands, not anyone else's.

Let's apply this idea to when someone tries to bully you. What thoughts and beliefs are starting to form in your mind? When the bully says something hurtful, can I control what they said? **No, I can't.** But I can learn to control how I react to it.

I can decide not to dwell on it, or I can begin to replay it over and over in my mind. Instead of letting those thoughts take over, you have the power to choose your response. Maybe you choose to avoid the person who is bullying you. You might be able to think about an appropriate response - perhaps something light or humorous - but you won't allow those negative thoughts to stay and control your mind and make you feel unhappy, fearful or anxious.

Bullies feed off your reactions. You don't have to give them that power. The bully may be getting reactions from others who think he's cool and funny, but you can't control what others do or think - **you can only control yourself.**

If he can't hurt you emotionally, then he can't truly bully you. Your emotional strength is yours to protect.

Not every problem in life can be dismissed so easily, but you can learn to stay positive and peaceful no matter what comes your way. It takes practice, but by consciously choosing your reactions, you can stop the cycle of negativity and protect your power and positivity.

I choose not to react. But this doesn't mean I become quiet or walk away feeling defeated. It doesn't mean I let myself look like a "loser" or shrink in the moment. It doesn't mean I drop my eyes and avoid looking at anyone.

Instead, I choose to **keep living my life**, staying focused on what I was doing, as if the comment or action never occurred. I refuse to give any emotional reaction. Keep your body language strong and confident. Continue to engage with the positive people around you, showing that you are unaffected. If you can effectively ignore a bully and refuse to respond emotionally - maybe even offering a brief, light-hearted humorous comment - you'll likely find that they quickly lose interest. Bullies thrive on reactions, but if they're not getting what they want, they often give up. By maintaining control over your response, you keep your power. Don't allow them to dictate your emotions or your behaviour. Rise above it.

Empowerment is not about controlling what others say or do, it's about **owning** and **controlling** your reaction to what others say or do. You will not overcome your bullying problem by trying to control the bully. You can't. True empowerment comes when we focus on our own responses and retain control over our actions and emotions, regardless of the behaviour of others.

Natural Skills are valuable.
Identify any natural skills and abilities you may possess that could help you cope with the bullying situation. Equally, reflect on how you are presenting yourself. How are others seeing you? This can offer valuable insights into things that you may need to address to become safer. Understanding and reading body language is a great skill.

Pay close attention to the following signs:

- **Confidence Levels**
  Do you present as timid, embarrassed or scared?

- **Eye Contact**
  Do you make eye contact comfortably, or do you avoid it, find yourself staring at the ground?

- **Body Language**
  How do you move? Do you walk with small, hesitant steps, with your head down and your shoulders hunched? Does your appearance make you feel weak?

- **Speech and Tone**
  How do you speak? Do you speak quietly or hesitantly, with an apologetic tone? Do you express opinions confidently? Do you speak up for yourself or do you lack the confidence to do so?

- **Power and Control**
  Do you know what you want for yourself? Have you tried to handle the situation on your own? Do you have a support network among your peers or do you feel alone?

- **Emotional State**
  How would you describe your emotional state? Are you angry, fearful or deeply scarred? Do you feel depressed? Can you identify any signs of resilience within you, are you able to bounce back quickly or do you struggle to recover lost confidence and self-esteem?

By paying attention to these factors, you can better understand your feelings and what support you may need. Ask a parent, a trusted adult or a friend to go through these questions with you. This may help you get a better understanding of how others may see you. This assessment will help guide your approach to building resilience and put you on the right path by identifying the things you will need to work on.

After making this assessment, focus on finding the needed support and take action. For some, this may involve working with someone who can provide long-term support, while others may be able to pick things up quickly and begin to move forward with less or even no assistance.

It's important to recognise that everyone's response to bullying is different and support should be tailored to the individual's needs. Whether it's a long-term plan or short-term guidance, the goal is to empower and help the person regain and retain control, confidence and a feeling of safety.

Practice Exercise 3: "I Choose to Take Control of My Thoughts"

Purpose:
To help you identify unhelpful thoughts and practice choosing positive, empowering responses instead of reacting negatively to bullying.

Exercise 3:

Part 1: Recognise the Thought Trap

> *"The first step to controlling my reactions is to notice what's going on in my mind."*

Think back to a time when someone said or did something that really upset you.
It might be something a bully said at school, online, or even a look or laugh that made you feel small or embarrassed.

- What did they do or say?
- How did it make you feel?
- What thoughts started running through your head?
- What did you do?

Example:

"They called me 'loser' in front of everyone. I felt humiliated. I kept thinking, everyone must think that's true. I hate myself. I should've said something. But I just looked down and walked away. I kept thinking about it over and over. I must have looked weak."

Part 2: Break the Cycle – "Don't Go There"

"I don't have to go down that path. I can choose a better one."

Now ask yourself:

- Did going over those thoughts help you feel better?
- What happened to your emotions after replaying the moment over and over?

Now try this:

Say quietly to yourself, **"Don't go there."**

Now say to yourself:

- "I can't control what they did, but I can control how I react to it."
- "I choose not to give them control over how I feel and live."
- "I choose to focus on what makes me strong and happy."

Part 3: Choose Your Focus

"Where attention goes, energy flows."

Think of **three things** that make you feel confident, safe and happy — things no bully can take away from you.

Examples:

- "I'm good at drawing."

- "I have a kind heart."
- "My dog wags his tail every time I come home."

Then say to yourself:

"This is who I am. This is what matters to me."

Part 4: Power Posture Practice

"Even how I stand and speak tells others that I respect myself."

Stand up. Take a deep breath.

Now practice:

- Standing tall with big shoulders
- Looking straight ahead (not down)
- Taking up and owning your space
- Saying to yourself with a calm, confident clear voice:
  " Don't go there, I'm in charge of me."

Try walking across the room with a sense of strength, calm and confidence, head up, walking and looking strong.

Part 5: Reflect and Plan

Now, answer these questions:

- What can I do next time someone tries to bully me?
- How can I remind myself not to react?
- Who can I talk to when I need help or support?

Remember:

"I cannot control the bully but I *can* learn to control me".

CHAPTER SIX

STANDING STRONG

The Power of Body Language

"If you look strong, you will begin to feel strong."

One of the most immediate and powerful ways to rise above bullying is to address negative body language. We often don't realise that our body language reveals how we feel about ourselves—sending messages that can either invite bullying or project the confidence needed to stand against it.

Ari was a Year 7 student who was struggling deeply. When I first met him, he was a shell of a person, weighed down by his emotions. Ari hated school, felt rejected by his classmates and thought he was the loneliest person on the planet. His parents had separated and the tension at home left him feeling like there was no one to turn to.

In the beginning, Ari had started Year 7 with some motivation. He had a few friends and school was his escape from the chaos at home. But as time went on, his so-called friends began to turn on him. What had once been a group he felt comfortable in, gradually became a group that used him as the butt of their jokes, isolating him and making him the target of fun and ridicule. The more this happened, the more Ari retreated. He stopped doing his schoolwork and interacting with others and began to withdraw into himself. He was so hurt by the bullying that it felt easier to shut everyone out. It wasn't long before he became a shadow of the boy who had once had a few friends. The more he isolated himself, the more the bullying escalated. And with that, his unhappiness grew. One day, after a particularly tough moment in class, Ari lashed out in frustration. He physically attacked another student, a reaction to the bullying he had been receiving. This landed him in trouble with his teacher and it felt like everything was falling apart.

When I started working with Ari, I spent time listening to him talk about his family, his struggles and the pain he carried. We worked through some of his emotional issues, but I realised there was something more at play. Ari wasn't just suffering from personal turmoil; he was also being bullied. I decided to dig deeper and it didn't take long before I discovered something surprising. Ari had a passion outside of school - he was involved in Cadets. At Cadets, Ari felt important. He was a leader, respected, liked, confident and happy. The same boy who walked around school with his shoulders slumped and head down was someone else entirely in that environment. That's when I decided to do something different. I needed to help Ari take that confidence he displayed at Cadets and bring it to school.

The Power of Body Language

When I first started working with Ari on his confidence, I realised that his body language was sending all the wrong messages. He didn't make eye contact with anyone. His gaze was always fixed on the floor, his shoulders were hunched and his movements were slow and lethargic. It was as if he was carrying the weight of the world on his shoulders. His body language was a reflection of how powerless and small he felt inside. This made him an easy target for the bullies.

I sat with Ari and shared a simple idea with him: **If you look strong, you will begin to feel strong.** I told him that we were going to work on his body language because it could change everything. We started with something simple - **standing tall.** I explained that strong body language didn't just come from being physically strong; it came from owning your space, presenting yourself as someone who deserves respect.

We practiced standing up straight, with his feet firmly planted on the ground, imagining roots that were connecting him to the earth - strong and unmovable. He would stand tall, lift his chin and look forward. We talked about how his body was like a shield. When he walked with confidence, he would stop inviting people to pick on him and start attracting respect instead. At first, it was hard for him. He was used to walking around with his head down, trying to disappear. But every time I saw him practicing, I could see the difference.

Making Eye Contact

The next part of the puzzle was eye contact. Ari was terrified of looking people in the eye, thinking that if he did, the bullies would target him even more. But in truth, avoiding eye contact made him appear weak and bullies could see that as an invitation to keep pushing him around. I had him practice eye contact. I told him, "Look at people like you are welcoming them into your world. Make eye contact with a friendly expression." We started with small steps, just looking at people's faces when he passed them in the hallway. And as time went on, I could see Ari starting to embrace the idea. His eyes started to change from fearful to friendly and he was beginning to understand that **strong friendly eyes** - eyes that communicated confidence - could stop bullies in their tracks.

Finding His Voice

The next challenge was his voice. At school, Ari spoke softly, almost apologetically, like he was afraid to take up space or be heard. But having strong body language wasn't enough if the voice didn't match it. I worked with him on how to use his voice to assert himself. We talked about the difference between aggression and assertiveness. Aggression might involve shouting or threatening, but assertiveness meant standing up for yourself firmly, without attacking others. We practiced some assertive lines, such as, "I don't appreciate that," and "That's not funny." Slowly but surely, Ari began to speak up more, his voice growing stronger as he realised he didn't have to be a doormat.

Making Friends

Even with Ari's newfound body language, he still faced challenges. He had trouble reconnecting with his peers. He felt as though he'd been so hurt by the bullying that he wasn't sure if it was worth the risk of trying to make new friends. I told him that if he was going to find happiness at school, he had to take risks, he had to let people in. He needed to be open to building friendships, even if it felt scary. Over time, I saw him take more risks, talking to others, joining in activities and slowly allowing himself to open up. It wasn't easy, but he was starting to get the hang of it.

The Transformation

One day, Ari came to me and said, "You know, I'm not the same person at school that I am at Cadets. I'm starting to feel like I can be that person here too." It wasn't an overnight change, but the transformation was happening. With each step, Ari's confidence grew. His body language had shifted from appearing weak and vulnerable, to strong, comfortable, confident and assertive. He was starting to feel strong on the inside because he had practiced looking strong on the outside. He was presenting himself as someone who deserved to be treated with respect.

By the end of the term, Ari was a different person. He wasn't just surviving at school; he was starting to thrive. The bullying had stopped, not just because we addressed the issue head-on, but because Ari had taken responsibility for how he presented himself to the world. His body language, his voice and his attitude had all changed and so had the way people treated him. Ari's story is evidence of the power of body language. **If you look strong, you will begin to feel strong.** And if you feel strong, you can stand up to anything life throws at you.

An important lesson is learning to stand strong and not show your fear. Bette Midlers's song "The Rose", features the line, "It's the soul afraid of dying – that never learns to live". Stand up to your fears and you will learn to live. The key is to keep your head high, maintain eye contact and never show the bully that you've been hurt. By standing strong and not giving in to fear, you will not only maintain your dignity but also send a strong message to the bully: "I won't be broken."

Learning to overcome bullying isn't just about stopping the bullying, it's about being empowered to protect your sense of self. With the right skills, you will become confident, resilient and unaffected by bullying behaviours. Over time, these skills can make a real difference in your ability to navigate social situations and feel safe in any environment. It's a journey of growth and every small success builds your confidence and ability to face challenges head-on.

Lessons to be taken from Ari's Story:

1. **Strong Body Language**
   - Standing tall, upright posture
   - Big shoulders, head up
   - Walking with strength and purpose

2. **Eye Contact**
   - Looking people in the eye with a calm, friendly expression

3. **Assertive Voice**
   - Speaking clearly and confidently
   - Using calm but firm language

4. **Willingness to Reconnect**
   - Taking risks to engage with others
   - Opening up and participating in social activities

5. **Taking Responsibility**
   - Owning how you present to the world
   - Practicing self-empowerment and resilience

Practice Exercise 4: "Standing Strong"

Purpose:
To help you feel more confident and reduce bullying by practicing strong body language, eye contact and assertive communication.

Step 1: The Power Stance
- Stand with feet shoulder-width apart
- Imagine strong roots growing from your feet into the ground
- Straighten your back, big shoulders and lift your chin slightly
- Breathe deeply and slowly

Say aloud (or in your head):
"I am strong. I deserve respect. I am standing tall like a tree. I am a big strong tree with roots that extend deeply into the ground. No storm can knock me over."

Repeat daily in front of a mirror.

Step 2: Practice Friendly Eyes – Be welcoming

What to do:
- Look into a mirror and meet your own eyes
- Hold the gaze for 5 seconds, then smile slightly
- Imagine you're greeting a friend.

Next level:
- Practice with a parent, teacher or trusted friend
- Look them in the eyes briefly (3–5 seconds) during a short conversation.

Goal: Eye contact that is welcoming, warm, friendly and confident.

Step 3: Find Your Voice

What to do:
Stand in your power stance and practice saying these lines out loud in a clear, steady voice:

- "I don't appreciate that."
- "Stop."
- "That's not okay"
- "Leave me alone"

Try this on others and get feedback on the strength of your voice.

Challenge: Practice your name and one sentence about yourself:

"Hi, I'm [your name] and I like [something you enjoy]."

Repeat this daily to build confidence using your voice.

Step 4: Daily challenge

Try one small social action:

- Say hi to someone you don't know
- Ask someone to join a game or sit near you
- Smile at someone as you walk past.

Reflect:

"Today I took a small risk by..."

Celebrate the attempt, not the outcome!

What part of "looking strong" has helped me feel stronger this week?

CHAPTER SEVEN

MASTERING SOCIAL SKILLS

Building Bridges

"Building on a solid foundation"

"Deep down, he wanted to be liked, accepted and to belong."

This chapter doesn't attempt to cover everything. Instead, I've kept the content simple and easy to follow, focusing on key, proven strategies that are easy to learn and share—whether you're a parent, teacher, counsellor or support person. Though straightforward, these techniques can have a powerful impact when used consistently. My goal is to lay a strong foundation for lasting change—empowering you to improve social skills and navigate interactions with greater confidence and success.

When I first met Vincent, he had built such high walls around himself that he could hardly remember what it felt like to belong. Like many people who have faced bullying, the need to connect and be accepted was still there, hidden beneath layers of hurt and anger. It's a desire we all share: to be part of something, to have friends and to feel safe. But for Vincent, this simple wish felt like an impossible dream.

Vincent's bullying issue had been successfully dealt with by the school, using the restorative program **Shared Responsibility**. This program, which encourages collaboration and understanding, allowed Vincent to feel supported and understood. However, while the bullying had stopped, Vincent accepted that there was more work to be done.

He was prepared to put in the extra effort to improve himself, but he also wanted to understand how he had ended up in that difficult situation in the first place.

Through our sessions, it became clear that Vincent's basic social skills were lacking. He didn't know how to make or keep friends. He didn't understand what it truly meant to be a friend. His past experiences with others had left him feeling isolated and unsure of how to interact in healthy, meaningful ways.

We began our work together with a few simple questions: "Can you think of someone you like? What is it about them that made them easy to be friends with?" At first, Vincent couldn't think of anyone. He sat in silence, almost as if the idea of friendship had slipped away from his world entirely. But then, after a moment of reflection, a memory surfaced. A boy from his primary school came to mind, a friend who had once made him feel accepted.

I asked Vincent what it was about this boy that had made him like him so much. And slowly, he shared:

- "He was friendly and nice"
- "He was fun to be with"
- "He talked to me, listened and shared things with me."

These three qualities - **friendliness, fun and communication** - form the foundation of all meaningful friendships. They're simple, but they're the key ingredients for connecting with others. And what we discovered was that Vincent, somewhere along the way, had stopped practicing them. He had withdrawn from the very things that could bring him closer to others.

To help Vincent rebuild his social connections, I guided him through a few exercises that demonstrated just how important each of these three elements is in forming lasting friendships.

The first exercise was about the importance of being friendly and nice. I asked Vincent to imagine a person who was fun and shared things, but wasn't always nice or friendly. Perhaps this person would ignore others when it suited him, or make fun of them in front of the group. It was clear that such behaviour wouldn't sustain a good friendship. Without being friendly and nice, any connection would break down.

The second exercise focused on the need for fun. I explained that, especially for teenagers, fun is essential to forming lasting bonds. What good is a friendship with someone who listens and talks but never joins in any fun? Without laughter, play or shared activities, friendships often fall flat. Vincent could see that someone who always remained down, refusing to participate, would be left out and forgotten. Learning to laugh again, to have fun, became a crucial part of his social recovery.

The third exercise centred on communication. What happens when someone is friendly, fun to be with, but never listens or really engages with others? We all know the type, the one who talks only about themselves, dominating conversations and ignoring others' thoughts and feelings. The person who never listens. This is where Vincent really began to understand how important it is not just to talk, but to listen and share equally. Without mutual respect and communication, friendships fall apart.

Through these exercises, Vincent came to realise that friendships are built on a balance of these three key ingredients: **being nice, having fun** and **engaging in meaningful, mutual conversation**.

Practicing the Art of Conversation

Now came the real work. I encouraged Vincent to reflect on his own ability to connect. I asked him questions like:

- "Do you think you are friendly and nice?"
- "Do you know how to have fun and are you fun to be with?"
- "Do you listen to others and show interest in what they say?"

Vincent admitted that he had become withdrawn and had stopped being nice or friendly. He was no longer fun to be around and his conversations had become stilted and awkward. We needed to change that.

We began by practicing and role-playing simple conversations, step by step. Each time we met, we would explore different scenarios, focusing on improving Vincent's conversation, friendliness and social skills. Our goal was to reach a point where Vincent could enter a meaningful, natural-flowing conversation and forget that he was even role-playing. We needed to create moments that felt authentic, as if they were real conversations happening in the moment.

Our practice began with straightforward scenarios:

- Sitting at a bus stop next to a stranger, and starting a casual conversation
- Welcoming a new person on their first day, making them feel at ease
- Navigating the experience of being the new student, learning how to make new friends and find out about the school
- Sitting next to someone at a football game, making small talk and enjoying the shared experience.

Each role-play was designed to build Vincent's confidence and social skills in different settings, encouraging him to feel comfortable and to speak naturally, allowing the conversations to flow with ease. With each session, Vincent's ability to engage improved, making it easier for him to connect in real-life situations.

We practiced listening skills, encouraging Vincent to pick up on clues that would keep the conversation going. For example, if someone mentioned a hobby, we would ask questions about that hobby, exploring what they liked about it and sharing a similar experience of his own, if he had one. Slowly but surely, Vincent learned to keep the conversation flowing, asking open-ended questions and expressing genuine interest.

One day, at the beginning of one of our sessions, I asked Vincent how things had gone at Fire Brigade the previous week. As he began replying, he suddenly stopped mid-sentence and smiled. "Wait a minute," he said, a lightbulb moment flashing in his eyes, "I just realised you've started another exercise, haven't you?" He chuckled, recognising that what had started as a simple conversation had once again evolved into one of our role-playing scenarios. It was a moment of clarity for Vincent, a sign that our practice had become so ingrained in his routine that he could now recognise the flow of a conversation and the purpose behind it, without even thinking twice. It was a small victory, but one that spoke volumes about how far he had come in learning and developing his social skills. Vincent was beginning to understand that conversations weren't just about talking, they were about connecting.

The Transformation

Vincent's transformation was gradual but profound. Over time, his body language became more confident. He smiled more, made eye contact and engaged with his classmates. He learned to listen actively, to find common ground with others and to share his own experiences in a way that made him relatable and likable.

After a few months, Vincent was a different person. His self-esteem had skyrocketed. He rated himself an 8 or 9 out of 10 on the happiness scale, a stark contrast to the 2 out of 10 he had rated himself when we first started working together. The bullying had stopped. Vincent no longer felt he was at the bottom of the social ladder. Instead, he found himself building real friendships and enjoying his time at school again. Though not every person in his class was his type of person, Vincent no longer felt like an outsider. He had found his place. And most importantly, he felt safe, confident and supported.

Not every person will need the same level of support and some may require different strategies. For some, this might mean ongoing counselling; for others, brief check-ins or group support might be enough. What's important is that every person has the opportunity to practice these key ingredients of friendship: being friendly, having fun and engaging in communication.

In schools where resources are limited, the **Shared Responsibility** model offers a path to success. Teachers, counsellors and support staff all have a role to play in helping people like Vincent build the confidence and skills they need to connect with others and thrive in the schoolyard.

Vincent's story is evidence that with the right support, every person can find their place. The journey may take time, but it's always worth it when a person steps into the light and says, "I now feel that I belong here."

Through Vincent's journey, I've highlighted the important role that developing good social skills plays in helping young people stay safe and recover from bullying. Bullies often prey on those with poor friendship and social skills, identifying them as easy targets to assert their power.

Parents can use these ideas with their children, creating opportunities to get closer and gain deeper understanding of their child's thoughts, feelings and their world. Likewise, teachers, counsellors, youth workers and chaplains can incorporate these practices into their work with young people, fostering stronger connections and a sense of belonging.

While the concepts may seem simple on the surface, don't underestimate their power. The process of improving social skills can be transformative, helping young people navigate the complex dynamics of school and life. Good social skills are a foundational tool for building confidence, resilience and the ability to form meaningful, supportive relationships. They are essential not only for fostering connection but also for staying safe in social environments. By cultivating these skills, young people are better equipped to navigate challenges, connect with others and build a network of positive relationships that support their wellbeing.

The example of Vincent's journey in "Mastering Social Skills: Building Bridges" highlights several key skills that were instrumental in helping him overcome the effects of bullying.

Identified Skills:

1. **Being Friendly and Nice:** Demonstrating genuine interest, warmth, and approachability towards others.
2. **Being fun:** Participating in enjoyable and shared experiences that foster connection.
3. **Engaging in meaningful Communication:** Balancing speaking and active listening to create mutual understanding and respect.
4. **Self-Reflection:** Assessing one's own social behaviours and their impact on relationships.
5. **Role-Playing and Practice:** Engaging in simulated social scenarios to build confidence and competence.

Practice Exercise 5: "The Three ingredients of a meaningful relationship"

Objective: To help develop and reinforce the foundational elements of building and maintaining friendships: kindness, shared enjoyment, and effective communication.

Materials Needed: Paper, pen/pencil and a partner (can be a friend, family member or mentor).

Steps:

1. **Write down the three steps:** Kindness," "Fun," and "Communication."

2. **Self-Assessment:**
   - Rate yourself on a scale of 1 to 5 for each one
     - **Kindness**: Do you show genuine interest and warmth towards others?
     - **Fun**: Do you engage in enjoyable activities with others?
     - **Communication**: How effectively do you balance speaking and listening in conversations?

3. **Identify Areas for Growth:**
   - Note which one has the lowest score. This will be your starting point for improvement.

4. **Role-Play Scenarios:**
   - With your partner, role-play situations that target your focus area. For example:
     - **Kindness**: Greeting a new classmate and inviting them to join a group activity
     - **Fun**: Planning a shared hobby or game to enjoy together – sharing jokes and funny stories
     - **Communication**: Practicing active listening by summarising what your partner shares before responding.

5. **Feedback and Reflection:**
   - After each role-play, discuss with your partner what went well and what could be improved.

6. **Practice Conversation:** Sit down with someone and practice being friendly by creating and maintaining a conversation. Choose a topic or get someone else

to choose one. Learn to listen, show interest in what they are saying by asking questions. Look at them so they know you are interested. Share your thoughts and knowledge. Be prepared to learn. Show interest in things that you may not be interested in.

7. **Real-Life Application:**
    - Set a goal to apply the practiced skill in a real-life situation within the next week
    - Afterward, reflect on the experience and note any changes in your interactions
    - Practice listening by identifying things shared and delving more deeply into it. Develop conversation skills.

By consistently practicing and reflecting on these core aspects of friendship, you will enhance your social skills, build stronger connections and build a supportive network that will assist you in rising above the effects of bullying.

CHAPTER EIGHT

TURN FEAR INTO STRENGTH

How do I build Confidence?

> *"Above all else, do not show your fear"*

This is advice I often give to those who might feel more vulnerable to bullying because of their gentle, quiet nature. Some individuals, through no fault of their own, have personalities that can attract negative attention. These are often the kind and reserved people who avoid confrontation and have a quiet, thoughtful, reflective demeanour. Unfortunately these very qualities, qualities that make them unique and valuable, can sometimes be interpreted as weakness and they become targets of bullies.

Some people seem to emit subtle, unconscious signals that can make them easy targets for bullies. These cues might include gentle body language, a quiet nature, a slower pace, a lack of energy, or a reluctance to make eye contact. These are not to be viewed as flaws, simply personality traits that can be complemented with practical tools to strengthen one's self-presentation and confidence. While no one should need to adjust themselves to avoid bullies, understanding these dynamics can be a useful safeguard. The goal isn't to change who they are but to empower them with a more resilient presence that helps them to be and stay safe.

With a little help and small shifts in self-presentation, they can appear more empowered and less vulnerable, confident and resilient.

Case Study: Josh

Student Support – The 'Victim' Student

Josh was not a 'wounded student' but he was a victim. Josh was being constantly picked on and made fun of. He was referred to the school youth worker because the school felt he could do with some support. Josh had trouble making friends, became angry easily, was often by himself and was subjected to frequent teasing. Josh had poor body language, was not sporty or trendy and when he wasn't being ignored, he was an object of fun and ridicule. The youth worker was given the basic information but the main objectives for the referral were never made clear. Josh was a typical 'victim student'. The youth worker worked with Josh regularly for about three months. He explored his family life, his schoolwork, his interests, his feelings, his anger, his fears and managed to assist Josh in many ways. Unfortunately, he did not teach Josh the skills he needed most. As a result, Josh continued to be a loner, feel unsafe, become angry easily and endure constant rejection and ridicule.

The School's Responsibility

The school had a responsibility to teach Josh and others like him how to be safe and feel safe at school. This means equipping them with tools to handle bullying when it happens and, more importantly, giving them the confidence to navigate their world.

Schools are more than just places for academic learning; they are training grounds for social skills and emotional resilience. In Josh's case, his issues with bullying could have been reduced if he had learned how to connect with peers, how to stand up for himself without confrontation and how to navigate complex social situations without retreating into anger or isolation.

But the truth is, teaching these skills isn't as easy as handing out a worksheet. These lessons are about complex personal development. It's about teaching students how to protect their sense of power, how to become and remain confident, unshaken and how to respond to others who may try to bully them.

As time passed, Josh continued to experience the same issues. He still had trouble making friends and still found himself being teased by the same group of students. He continued to get angry easily and isolate himself. The youth worker had done his best, but without teaching Josh the key skills for coping with bullies, he remained stuck in the same cycle.

Josh isn't the only one like this. There are countless others who, for various reasons, seem to invite bullying behaviour simply by the way they carry themselves, the way they interact with others or their inability to navigate the social complexities of teenage life.

Breaking the Cycle

The first step in helping a person like Josh is to teach them to recognise how their reactions feed into the bullying. A bully's power is largely based on the victim's reactions. When a person reacts with anger or shows that they're upset, they give the bully the reaction they're seeking. When a student successfully ignores the bullying, disengages from the situation and shows no sign of hurt, the bully loses power.

The best way to approach this is to start by teaching them how to block out hurtful words. Teenagers in particular are naturally skilled at tuning out information, whether it's a teacher's instructions or a parent's request. But for some reason, when it comes to bullying, they tune in to every insult and every cruel word. It seems they can't help but listen, absorb and internalise the hurt.

The aim here is to help people retrain their minds to ignore those words. "What you don't hear can't hurt you. If you can ignore your teacher's boring lecture or your parents' requests, you can ignore a bully's insulting words." It sounds simple, but it does work. When people learn to mentally tune out the insults, they are less likely to be impacted emotionally. And when they stop reacting, the bully loses power and interest.

Another strategy I use with people is the concept of the 'happy place.' This idea comes from the movie Happy Gilmore, where the main character learns to control his temper by imagining a place where he feels safe and happy. The idea is to teach students how to mentally escape the bullying situation. When they feel attacked by bullying, they can go to their 'happy place', an imaginary place where they feel relaxed, safe, peaceful and happy.

I'll often ask people to picture themselves in a place where they're doing something they love. It could be playing their favourite game, spending time with family or friends, or just sitting by the ocean. This helps them create a mental buffer between themselves and the bullying, potentially reducing the impact of the bully.

Josh's story, like so many others, underscores the importance of a multi-faceted approach to bullying. It's not enough to address individual incidents; we must equip people with the tools they need to stand strong in the face of adversity.

Learn how to:

- Block out hurtful words
- Retreat to a mental 'happy place'
- Practice assertiveness and maintain their dignity.

These strategies are not about changing who they are but about helping them become stronger versions of themselves. With time, teaching, practice and support, people like Josh can move from being targets of bullying to confident individuals capable of navigating the complexities of adolescence with resilience and confidence.

Key Skills Identified

1. **Emotional Regulation** - Learning to manage emotional responses, such as anger or sadness, to prevent giving bullies the reactions they seek.
2. **Mental Resilience Techniques** - Employing strategies like visualising a personal 'happy place' to create a mental buffer against bullying incidents.

3. **Assertiveness Training** - Developing the ability to stand up for oneself confidently and respectfully, without aggression.
4. **Non-Reactive Communication** - Practicing calm and composed responses to bullying, thereby reducing the bully's perceived power.
5. **Confidence-Building Practices** - Engaging in activities and exercises that enhance self-esteem and self-worth.

Practice Exercise 6: "Confidence Shield"

This exercise is designed to help build confidence and resilience, making them less susceptible to bullying.

Step 1: Visualise Your 'Happy Place'
- Close your eyes and take deep breaths
- Imagine a place where you feel safe, happy and relaxed. It could be a beach, a forest or any place you love
- Spend a few minutes immersing yourself in this environment, noting the sights, sounds and feelings associated with it (meditation – relaxing).

Step 2: Develop Assertive Responses
- Think of common bullying scenarios you might face
- For each scenario, practice assertive responses. For example:
    - If someone teases you, calmly say, "I don't appreciate that comment. Please stop."
    - If someone tries to provoke you, respond with, "I'm not interested in engaging in this conversation."

Step 3: Role-Playing

- With a trusted friend, family member or counsellor, role-play different bullying scenarios

- Practice maintaining eye contact, using a firm tone and stand tall

- After each role-play, discuss what went well and what could be improved.

Step 5: Engage in Confidence-Building Activities

- Participate and stay involved in activities that you enjoy and excel at, such as sports, arts or clubs

- These activities can help you build friendships and improve self-esteem.

By consistently practicing these steps, you can build a 'confidence shield' that not only deters bullies but also fosters a positive self-image and emotional resilience.

CHAPTER NINE

HUMOUR AS ARMOUR

Building Resilience in the Face of Bullying

"The goal is to empower"

Frankie was a Year 7 boy, sensitive to many things. He would often cry and ask, *"Why do they do this to me?"* One of Frankie's biggest frustrations was having his path deliberately blocked by other students. Whenever he tried to walk somewhere, others would deliberately move to block his path. When Frankie tried to walk around them, they would move to the side to block him again, causing Frankie great distress and leaving him in tears. This quickly became a popular game at school. Students would say, *"Watch me make this kid cry."*

After a few sessions with Frankie, I arranged to meet him in a classroom at lunchtime and made sure to arrive before him. When he arrived, I opened the door and deliberately stood in his way. As he tried to walk around me, I mirrored his movements, making it difficult for him to get past. Soon, Frankie was unknowingly playing a little game of cat and mouse, weaving, pushing, dodging and finally crawling through my legs to enter the room. He bounced around, proudly proclaiming his "victory" boasting about his success. I asked him, *"What did I just do?"* It took him a moment to realise that I had been doing exactly what had been upsetting him for so long. So why did he laugh and play with me, yet get distressed and upset when others did the same thing?

We can help shift a person's perspective by teaching them to deflect bullying attempts with humour and a sense of fun. Developing this skill is a valuable tool, particularly when responding to teasing. When we learn to laugh at ourselves and share in the joke with others, it can take the sting out of moments when someone tries to bully us. Of course, some remarks are genuinely painful and can't simply be laughed off, but many can. Cultivating the ability to laugh is not only a way to navigate challenging situations but is an essential part of building friendships and being happy.

Rather than being or feeling defensive about our differences, we should learn to celebrate them. After all, our differences make us unique and define who we are.

In that moment with Frankie, I asked him if he knew what a "blind turn" was. It's a move in Australian Rules Football where a player runs straight at an opponent and, just before making contact, rolls around them to get past. Frankie nodded, saying he knew the move, so we practiced it a few times. I suggested that he try this in the yard the next time someone tries to block his path.

It didn't take long for Frankie to be presented with an opportunity. Back in the yard, a student tried to block his path. With a sense of fun and confidence, Frankie walked straight toward the person, then performed a blind turn around them and kept going, raising his arm in victory as he passed. In that moment, Frankie transformed from being a victim to a hero. The students all thought it was funny and it became the new game for a short time.

Deflection Skills using Humour

Humour can be a powerful defence and deflection against bullying. It's much harder to hurt someone who is laughing and having a good time. Humour is a powerful tool for de-escalating tension and silencing a bully. However, it must be used with caution and wisdom. The joke must be directed at yourself or the topic the bully has chosen, but never directed as an attack at the bully. This will only cause confrontation and become an invitation for the bully to engage in a battle for power.

For the person with a good sense of humour this idea is worth experimenting with. Many a bully has been silenced and put in their place by a quick-thinking comeback that makes people laugh. It also important to note that the comeback needs to be delivered as a joke, in a joking, non-aggressive manner. It's intended to make people laugh, not antagonise them.

Humour, when used skilfully, can defuse aggression and break the tension in moments of bullying. It offers a powerful tool for both the person being targeted and for any bystanders, helping everyone involved to feel less threatened and more at ease.

Research has shown that those who are able to use humour to diffuse a bullying situation often demonstrate greater resilience in times of stress and adversity throughout life. Humour creates a sense of emotional distance from the pain of bullying, making it easier to endure challenging moments.

Beyond this, humour fosters connection. Shared laughter strengthens bonds and can even transform hostile interactions, with the potential to turn bullies into friends.

When the person being bullied is able to laugh at themselves in a light-hearted way, it can disarm the bully, preventing their insults from having the intended impact. This response also projects confidence, subtly challenging the bully's power. Light, non-offensive jokes or witty comebacks can successfully shift the tone of an interaction.

When using humour as a deflection, it's important to be mindful of cultural differences. Humour that resonates in one cultural context may not translate well in another and could even risk escalating tensions. Sensitivity to these differences is crucial for ensuring that humour defuses rather than fuels conflict. Humour in a group setting that involves friends or allies can be especially effective. Bullying often seeks to isolate its target, but a united front expressed through shared laughter can significantly diminish the bully's power. If the observers laugh, the humour has likely been effective.

Staying calm is essential when using humour to deflect bullying. If humour is delivered with anger or frustration, it may come across as sarcastic or defensive rather than light-hearted and effective. Humour that highlights the absurdity of the situation, rather than targeting the bully directly, is the way to go. Ultimately, humour should aim to uplift, not belittle and create opportunities for connection.

Once a person recognises and learns how humour can diffuse bullying, they can apply it in their own situations. For example, if they're called a name like 'fat', responding with light-hearted humour has the potential to disarm the bully. Replies like, 'Who told you? They promised they wouldn't tell,' or 'Yeah, watch out I don't sit on you' convey confidence and show that the insults didn't bother you. A potential bully might become a good friend by laughing with him, claiming equal power in the banter. Fun makes friends.

If you have a good sense of humour, explore how you might use it to deflect potential bullying. Not all things can be, nor should be, laughed at but a lot of things can.

Here are some examples using humour to deflect a bullying comment. See if you can make them work for you. Change the wording to suit yourself.

> **Bully:** "Hey what's with you, it looks like you were just dragged out of bed."
>
> **Response:** "Hey, it's the new style. We call it 'bed hair' it's the new craze – get with it".
>
> **Bully:** "Hey, look what is she wearing? Hey Raggedy Anne"!
>
> **Response:** "Do you like it? it's called **'I don't care' fashion**. You should try it sometime."

Bully: "Hey look what she written? How smart is she"?

Response: "Yep, this is my entry for the 'Dumbest answer' award. You should enter".

Bully: "You don't have to answer every question; you think you know everything".

Response: "Yes, I do, I like to keep my brain active. You should try it sometime."

Bully: "Hey Stretch, don't knock your brains out going through that door".

Response: "It's okay, I know that I'm a giraffe in a room full of meerkats. I do come in handy when you have to get something off the top shelf".

Bully: "What Frankenstein, you never heard of the Beatles?"

Response: "Nup, I guess I've been living under a rock. I need to get out more. You know, up until last week I thought TikTok was an alarm clock!"

Bully: "Why don't you talk normal like us, ya wog"?

Response: "You think I sound funny now, just wait until I start talking through my bum".

Bully: "Look, the Nerd has finally decided to come to school. Mummy forget to wake me up, did she"?

Response: "No, dad's space ship broke down and I had to use my time machine to get here. Sorry, the future's a little tricky to navigate."

Bully: "I'd just love to be a Geek like you – GEEK!"

Response: "That would be Mr Geek to you sir. I prefer that people use my full title".

I encourage you to practice humour as a defence in a safe environment. This can be done with parents, friends, in workshops, in group work and role-playing activities where participants respond to mock bullying situations with humour. This can be a good laugh.

Another effective way to deflect bullying with humour is to get the person being bullied to laugh. This approach works best with a second person as an ally. For example, when a bullying remark is made, the two people, one being the target, look at each other and start laughing without revealing what they're laughing about.

I once worked with two girls eager to try this tactic, though they initially worried they couldn't produce a genuine laugh on cue. To help, I suggested they imagine their teacher bursting through the door on a unicycle, wearing nothing but their underwear. The girls instantly erupted in laughter. They even developed a signal, scratching their heads, to launch into laughter whenever one of them felt targeted.

The girls enjoyed this strategy so much that they nearly turned the tables, as the bully became increasingly embarrassed, having no idea what they found so funny. Eventually, the boy stopped bothering them altogether. The girls had such fun with it though, that I eventually had to intervene to ensure they didn't take it too far!

If you're considering humour as a tool against bullying, this chapter provides plenty of ideas to experiment with. The possibilities for humour are nearly endless. If something doesn't work or feels uncomfortable, don't worry, simply try a different approach. This book offers a wide range of strategies, all of which have proven effective for young people in real-life situations. Some methods may work better for certain individuals, while others may find success with different tactics. Choose what works for you.

Some people have formed friendships simply by embracing a nickname they've been given. However, others may find themselves isolated by taking offense or showing hurt. For instance, one boy I knew was fine with his close friends calling him "Porka" but he didn't like it if someone outside his group used it. In a sense, his own bias unintentionally was creating a barrier. If it was acceptable for some people to call him "Porka," why not everyone?

Many bullying scenarios can be defused, or even avoided, with light-hearted replies, such as:

- **"You're gay."**
  Response: "Who told you? They promised they wouldn't tell!"

These types of responses should be practiced to ensure they remain light-hearted, friendly and non-confrontational. Often, the best comebacks come naturally - they just need a supportive and relaxed environment to emerge.

Not everyone finds it easy to laugh off offensive remarks. For those people, it's crucial to explore alternative strategies for coping with and countering the effects of bullying.

Summary:

1. **Understanding Your Reactions**
   Recognising how your reactions influence a bully's behaviour is crucial. Bullies often seek a visible response; by managing your emotions, you can reduce their impact.

2. **Using Humour as a Deflection Tool**
   Humour can be a powerful way to diffuse tension. Responding to teasing with a light-hearted joke can disarm the bully and show that their words don't affect you.

3. **Practising Assertive Body Language**
   Standing tall, making eye contact, and speaking confidently can deter bullies by projecting self-assurance.

Practice Exercise 7:   "Experiment with Humour"

New Skills to Build Confidence and Deflect Bullying

Objective: To develop the ability to respond to bullying with confidence and humour.

Materials Needed: A trusted friend, family member or counsellor to role-play scenarios with you.

Steps:

1. **Think of a time when you were bullied**
   Identify an incident where you've felt bullied e.g. someone mocking your appearance or interests.

2. **Explore some Humorous Responses**
   Create light-hearted comebacks that deflect the insult without escalating the situation. For instance:
   - Bully: "Nice outfit!" You: "Thanks! I was going for 'fashionably unique' today."
   - Bully: "You're such a nerd. "You: "Absolutely! Nerds are the future, after all."

3. **Role-Play the Scenario with a friend or parent**
   Act out the bullying situations and practice delivering your responses confidently. Focus on being funny.

4. **Reflect and Adjust**
   After each role-play, discuss what felt effective and what could be improved. Adjust your responses and delivery as needed.

5. **Practice Regularly**
   Regular practice can help make these responses more natural, so you're prepared if a real situation arises. Practice using humour in a safe environment with your friends. Chances are that you are already doing it.

Remember, the goal isn't to change who you are, but to equip you with tools to handle challenging situations confidently. By understanding your reactions, using humour and practising assertive responses, you can reduce the impact of bullying and protect your self-esteem.

CHAPTER TEN

THE POWER OF IGNORING – FROM ACTING TO REALITY

Acting Strong: Using Drama to Build Resilience Against Bullying"

"Drama - is the art of pretending"

"Drama is the art of pretending, of stepping into a role, embodying a character or expressing an emotion. You might need to act joyful and laugh, or you might need to look sad and upset. Sometimes you'll need to pretend you're hurt and limp, or stand tall, projecting strength and confidence. Drama can be a powerful tool in dealing with bullying: **When you look strong, you start to feel strong.**"

Drama allows you to practice responses in a safe, controlled environment. Through role-playing and pretending, you learn to project confidence and resilience, even if you don't feel it. This "acting" skill helps you manage your reactions, which can reduce a bully's power. Over time, acting will not be required as the pretending will be transformed into reality. To successfully portray a strong and confident person, you must fully embrace the role - appearing, feeling, acting and immersing yourself into the character. If you need to cry, you must genuinely internally connect with the emotion to make it convincing. You must feel the real sadness. Similarly, if the role demands acting unbothered, you must feel and project the confidence and strength to make it work.

Drama is a strategy that has helped many people overcome the effects of bullying. If I can't laugh things off, I can act as if I can. If I haven't yet reached the point where things don't bother me, I can act as if I have. Drama allows people to work on presentation, body language - like standing tall, maintaining steady eye contact and using a firm tone of voice. Over time, these acted responses become natural and convincing, helping the person to project strength, which discourages bullies.

I encourage you to understand the value of projecting confidence and staying focused on your own activities when faced with bullying attempts. Bullies thrive on getting a reaction, so maintaining composure can deprive them of the response they're looking for. Some people believe they've effectively ignored a bully, yet they may still be giving away their power through subtle unconscious reactions. True resilience lies in staying calm and fully engaged, signalling that the bully's attempts have no real impact.

Ayhan was part of a group conversation when another person directed a bullying remark his way: *"And so, what did you do, 'goop'? Have a cry?"* Although Ayhan tried to ignore the comment, he unknowingly gave away his power by his reaction. He believed he did nothing, but in reality, he withdrew from the conversation, went silent, became a hurt observer on the edge of the group. This is not effective ignoring.

Stay connected and engaged:

Let bullying comments pass you by without showing signs of hurt or impact.

Possible responses could be:

- Completely ignore the comment and **stay engaged in the conversation or activity**
- Give a strong glance of disapproval toward the bully and **stay engaged in the conversation or activity**
- Make an assertive statement of disapproval and **stay engaged in the conversation or activity**
- Deflect the comment with humour and **stay engaged in the conversation or activity**.

Each of these options reinforces a stance of resilience by keeping active and engaged in the group.

The key is to stay engaged or to re-engage quickly. You might stay engaged by asking someone in the group a question, or you may comment on the topic being discussed, signalling that the remark did not hit its mark. This approach helps maintain your position in the group and shows resilience, sending a message that you are not impacted by the attempt to bully. If you are not engaged in a conversation at the time, it is important to keep doing what you were doing as if nothing was said.

A group might be discussing a football match played last weekend when a bullying comment is made.

Bullying remark: *"What would you know about football Smiffy – You can't play football."*

IGNORE: If Smiffy chooses to ignore it, then he lets it pass without a response, but he must make an effort to remain or take part in the conversation. **Stay engaged.**

Response: *"Hey Barry, what do you think of that goal Tarrant kicked in the third quarter?"*

LOOK OF DISAPPROVAL: Alternatively, Smiffy could make strong eye contact with the bully, just long enough to communicate *"not funny,"* before re-engaging in the conversation.

Response: *"Hammo, now what was I saying? Oh yeah, that umpire's decision near the end of the game..."*

ASSERTIVE RESPONSE: Smiffy might assertively address the comment before returning to the group discussion.

Response: *"Not funny. You'd do better to keep those comments to yourself or direct them at someone who cares."* Immediately **Re-engage** *"Hammo, now what was I saying? Oh yes, that umpire's decision at the end of the game..."*

HUMOUR: Smiffy might decide on a light-hearted humorous response,

Response: *"I can play many things, but I'm best at playing the clown."* Then immediately **Re-engage** – *"the outcome of the game wasn't impacted by the umpire."*

It is important not to engage the bullying student in conversation.

Here are a few more examples:

Ignoring or Walking Away:

Scenario: A person is being taunted. "Hey dickhead."

Response: Walk away without reacting, head up, looking strong with confidence and energy pretending that you did not hear it.

Assertive Responses:

Scenario: A person is called a derogatory name. *"Hey Camel face."*

Response: *"I don't appreciate that. Please don't say that again."*

Humour and Light-hearted Response:

Scenario: A person is teased about their appearance. "Look at what she's wearing today?"

Response: *"I guess I was born to stand out! Thanks for noticing".*

Empathy or Understanding Responses:

Scenario: A person is made fun of for being different. "Hey, how come you don't look like everybody else?"

Response: *"I understand that people might not get me, but that's okay. We all have our own things."*

All of these responses help you build confidence and prepare for similar situations in the future. It's essential to practice them while paying attention to key elements like tone, body language and eye contact. The way a response is delivered can significantly impact its effectiveness.

If bullying occurs during a class or group activity, the person must remain engaged and avoid becoming isolated. Bullying is most effective when it succeeds in separating the victim from the group. To counter this, the person should make every effort to stay connected, participating actively, while avoiding any signs of being wounded or giving away their power. Remaining engaged without reacting emotionally helps to maintain control of the situation and prevents the bully from gaining any power over you.

Endure with dignity:

If you find yourself in a position where you are having to endure bullying, do so with dignity. I often use the movie scenario of a tough hero facing overwhelming odds. He is being held captive by two men, one on each arm while a third gangster punches him in the stomach and face. Despite his struggle to escape and fight back, the captive is helpless. Yet, even in his captivity, he suffers with dignity. He keeps his head high and looks his assailants in the eye, sending a message with his gaze: "You can break my body, but you can't break my spirit." He bleeds with dignity, surrenders no power and stands strong, demonstrating that even in the face of physical or emotional assault, his inner strength remains untouchable.

Bullying is about breaking a person's spirit - it seeks to strip away their worth, power and self-esteem. Power and self-respect are mental states and they should be protected at all costs. *"What if they hit me?"* What if they do? What's worse: suffering in fear, feeling small and powerless, or getting a sore nose and bleeding with dignity? Your nose will heal in a few days, but a broken spirit may never fully recover.

Research has shown, very few bullies escalate their activities to include physical violence. They typically target those they believe can't defend themselves. This is the nature of a bully, they are cowards. When a person's reactions send a clear message of resistance, through confidence and resolve, the bully is more likely to look for someone else to bully.

If you cannot stop the bullying on your own, you are entitled to seek help. I encourage you to take action and get support, this is not a sign of weakness; rather it is a demonstration of strength. It takes courage to stand up for yourself and doing so is an important step in taking control of your situation. No one should have to endure bullying alone and seeking help is a powerful way to put an end to it. Reporting it to the school, the police or cyber police is encouraged where necessary.

These are all tactics you can use to use to stay safe and protect your power. My advice to all people is simple: stand strong, look strong, stay engaged and above all, do not show your fear.

We must take responsibility for our own wellbeing and be willing to take a few risks. If something doesn't work, try something else. Don't give up.

Practice using these strategies with siblings, friends and non-threatening peers in a safe environment. Each success, no matter how small, builds skill and confidence. Set yourself tasks. Start with smaller challenges, experiment with less threatening situations then gradually build up to more difficult ones. If something feels too hard, ease off and allow time for growth at your own pace. Talk with someone about your successes and failures. Talk about what it was that made that difficult for you? Even in a failure you might remind yourself that it took a lot of courage just to try.

Summary of Skills Illustrated in this Chapter

1. **Role-Playing and Drama Techniques:** Utilising drama to practice responses in a safe environment helps individuals prepare for real-life situations.
2. **Assertive Communication:** Responding to bullying with clear, confident statements without aggression.

3. **Do not show your hurt:** Maintaining composure and not showing hurt or anger.
4. **Stay Engaged:** Continuing participation in group activities despite bullying attempts.

Practice Exercise 8: "Building Your Resilience Through Role-Play"

Objective: To develop assertive communication and emotional regulation skills in response to bullying.

Materials Needed:
- A mirror or a recording device (e.g. smartphone)
- A trusted friend or family member to role-play with (optional)

Steps:

1. **Identify Common Scenarios:**

Think of situations where you've experienced or witnessed bullying. For example:
- Being teased about appearance
- Being called derogatory names

2. **Develop Assertive Responses:**

For each scenario, write down a calm and confident response. Examples:
- "I don't appreciate that comment. Please stop."
- "That's not funny. Let's keep the conversation respectful."

3. **Practice in Front of a Mirror:**
- Stand tall with big shoulders
- Maintain eye contact with your reflection
- Speak with a clear and firm tone

- Repeat your assertive responses, focusing on making them more effective.

4. **Record and Review:**
   - Record yourself practicing the responses
   - Watch the playback to observe your body language
   - Note areas for improvement and adjust accordingly.

5. **Role-Play with a Trusted Person:**
   - Have them act as the bully, delivering the teasing or derogatory comments
   - Respond with your practiced assertive statements
   - Use all the four suggested strategies and gauge what works best for you. (Ignore, Strong glance, assertive and humour).
   - Ask for feedback on your delivery and demeanour.

6. **Reflect and Adjust:**
   - After each practice session, reflect on what felt natural and what didn't.
   - Make necessary adjustments to your responses and practice again.

7. **Practice strong eyes** that say "not funny"
8. **Consider joining a drama or acting group.**

Tips:

- Consistency is key. Regular practice will build confidence
- Start with less challenging scenarios and gradually move to more difficult ones
- Remember, the goal is to respond assertively, not aggressively.

By consistently practicing these steps, you can enhance your ability to respond to bullying with confidence and resilience.

CHAPTER ELEVEN

ONLINE BULLYING

What can I do about cyberbullying?

The Path to Cyber Resilience

> *"Ignore, Block, Report, Don't go there"*

Online bullying is a serious issue affecting many people today. Cyberbullies, shielded by the anonymity of a screen, often act more aggressively than they might in person, further empowered by the distance the internet provides. Unfortunately, those targeted can also feel brave and empowered to respond, sometimes getting drawn into arguments, retaliation or online wars. But in the realm of online bullying, engagement only fuels the problem.

Cyberbullying requires a different approach as face-to-face strategies don't fit the mould. However, when you're out in the world, remember: **look the way you want to feel, don't let the way you feel dictate the way you look.** Walk confidently, with energy and purpose and keep your head held high. If a person who has posted something about you online sees you in the street, act as if you haven't read it. Projecting strength can help you feel stronger inside. If you've been cyberbullied, it's natural to feel down and those feelings may show in your body language. Make a conscious effort to keep your body language strong at all times. This can help you rebuild and overcome any hurt.

Avoid letting online bullying consume your thoughts. Rehashing hurtful messages intensifies the distress caused by cyberbullying. **DON'T GO THERE!** Train yourself to direct your mind away from hurtful comments and focus on the positive people and experiences in your life. Go to your happy place. Discipline your thoughts, stay centred on your happiness and don't let negativity creep in. Avoid letting your mind dwell on questions like who, what or why, as this only fuels negative emotions and deepens the pain within you. Cyberbullies want your attention, don't give it to them. This was covered in more detail in chapter 5.

Pictures, comments, accusations and humiliating stories can spread rapidly through cyberspace, drawing everyone's attention. The urge to fight back, explain your side or retaliate is natural, but doing so will only fuel the fire and make things worse. People will believe and share what they want. Unfortunately, you can't do anything about it. Stay disciplined, resist the temptation to engage and don't feed the drama.

It's easy for me to say, I'm not the one dealing with it. I know it hurts. You can report it, you can block it, but beyond that, there's little you can do without feeding it and making it worse. That's exactly what the bullies want. They want to get inside your head, embarrass you, provoke your anger and make you strike back or run away. They are on a power trip and any reaction or response feeds it. Unfortunately, this is one of the darker, more harmful aspects of the internet.

If you are being cyberbullied stay engaged in your usual activities and routine. Keep going to the places you normally go, continue interacting with the people you usually see, continue to hang out with your friends and don't retreat or isolate yourself. Life goes on as normal. If your friends bring it up, don't feel obligated to discuss it. Just say something like, **"I'm not interested, I don't need it, nor do I care."** This lets you maintain control without being rude. Stay happy, fun, and energetic. This becomes easier when you're not letting negativity dominate your thoughts. Remember, you have control over what you choose to focus on.

Four Steps to Freedom: **Don't Engage – Block - Report – Don't go there.**

The best advice I can give for dealing with online bullies is straightforward: *Don't engage, block, report and don't go there.* These four steps are simple but effective.

1. **Don't Engage:** Responding to bullies only gives them what they want - attention. Bullies thrive on people's reactions. No matter how tempting it may feel, resist the urge to defend yourself or retaliate. By staying silent, you maintain control and deny them the satisfaction of a reaction.

2. **Block:** Most social media platforms have a block feature. Use it. Blocking the bully stops them from contacting you and removes their comments from your view. You can't control what they think or post, but you *can* control what you do about it.

3. **Report:** Almost every platform has options to report abusive content. Reporting may feel like a small action, but it adds up and helps platforms take appropriate measures to keep online spaces safe.

4. **Don't Go there:** Often, we begin to replay what they said or did, thinking it over until it consumes our thoughts. Our minds start traveling down paths of anger, retaliation and revenge. The more we harbour these thoughts, the stronger and more consuming the negative emotions become. We can control what we choose to focus on in our minds. Since our goal is happiness and peace, we consciously decide not to go there. We don't take the bait. When the hurt and anger hit us, we tell ourselves, **"Don't go there."** We make a clear decision not to dwell on it, because we know where it will take us.

Self-discipline is key. You may feel curious to know what the bully is saying or what others might be hearing about you. Resist this curiosity. If friends try to tell you about hurtful comments they've seen, kindly but firmly tell them you're not interested. Knowing what has been said can intensify the emotional impact. Remind yourself: *DON'T GO THERE!* This may sound simple, but it's powerful.

Online bullying has become so widespread that many people now question the credibility of almost everything they see online. Most gossip and accusations are exaggerated or outright false and those with a good understanding of online dynamics take such posts with a grain of salt.

However, the greatest damage isn't in what others think, it's in how these posts affect you.

The harm lies in the impact on your mental health, self-confidence, emotions and overall sense of wellbeing. Cyberbullying can make you feel overwhelmed, isolated or even powerless, but it's crucial to remember that you have control over how you respond. While you can't control what others say or do online, you can control what you do about it.

Stay grounded, seek support, focus on your inner resilience, protect your power and rise above any potential harm.

Building Mental Resilience:

As with face-to-face bullying, ignoring is often the most powerful tool you have in your kitbag. Focus your energy on positive connections.

In cyberbullying situations, assertive responses, humour or deflection aren't needed nor are they helpful. *No response is the best response.* Anything you say can give the bully a new angle to use against you. Avoid the temptation to play their game; don't give them the satisfaction of pulling you in. Don't go there.

Summary: In addressing cyberbullying, several key skills are essential for building resilience and maintaining well-being:

Skills for Combating Cyberbullying

1. **Emotional Self-Discipline:** Resisting the urge to retaliate or dwell on negative comments.
2. **Digital Boundaries:** Utilising platform tools to block and report bullies, thereby limiting their access to you.
3. **Cognitive Redirection:** Actively steering thoughts away from harmful content and focusing on positive aspects of life.
4. **Routine Engagement:** Continuing daily activities and social interactions to prevent isolation.

These skills align with research emphasising the importance of resilience and proactive coping strategies in mitigating the effects of cyberbullying.

Practice Exercise 9: "Digital Resilience Drill"

Objective: To reinforce skills that help individuals manage and overcome the impact of cyberbullying.

Step 1: Scenario Simulation
- Imagine receiving a hurtful message online.

Step 2: Emotional Check-In
- Identify immediate emotional reactions (e.g. anger, sadness).

Step 3: Apply the "Four Steps to Freedom"
1. **Don't Engage**: Refrain from responding to the message.
2. **Block**: Use platform settings to block the sender.
3. **Report**: Report the message to the platform administrators.

4. **Don't Go There**: Avoid revisiting the message or ruminating on its content.

Step 4: Positive Reinforcement

- Stay engaged in activities that make you happy (e.g. listening to music, talking to a friend, playing sport, going out etc.)

- Continue to live your life.

CHAPTER TWELVE

THE ROAD TO RESILIENCE

How can I stand up and be strong?

Developing Assertiveness and Resilience

*"Self-control – Assertion – Mediation –
Self-defence – Becoming Bullyproof"*

Some people present as more angry and annoyed than distressed or isolated when being bullied. They are not 'wounded' nor are they 'a victim'. They generally walk, talk and present confidently. They explain the situation with controlled emotions and have no problems in talking with an adult. They can explain what they have tried to do to combat the bullying and they are willing and appear capable of trying other things to overcome the situation. They have become annoyed and don't know what to do other than ending up in a fight. These people don't fear the bullies. They simply have had enough. They function well within the community without fear or feelings of isolation. All they really need is a few strategies and ideas to respond and overcome the bullying themselves. Many of the strategies outlined in the previous chapters can point this person in the right direction.

Teach and rehearse some assertive responses such as:

"I don't want trouble, but if you continue to try and bully me, I'll have to do something about it", or
"This is starting to really annoy me. Not funny anymore!"

Another response that has proven effective is a strong and firm 'STOP' or 'NO'. "I'm not going to be bullied by you or anyone else for that matter. Find someone else to bully". This becomes even more powerful when delivered with strong eye contact and a strong 'STOP' hand signal. Practice saying this with and without the hand signal and discuss the difference. Talk about the power of both with a parent, friend or trusted adult.

Statements such as these need to be rehearsed and delivered with conviction or they will be laughed off. You should have a good idea if you have the ability to deliver them effectively. I'm sure you could do it convincingly with a brother or sister.

A confident person may decide to confront the bully and talk the matter through. If this is the case it is important that they don't confront a group. There is little chance the tormentor will back down or lose face in the presence of their peers. The numbers and the power will be strongly against you in this setting. On the other hand, away from the group, the tormentor has less to lose and is more likely to listen and assist. You may need some assistance in arranging to meet and talk privately with the bully. Decide what you want to achieve, what you want to say and the best way to say it. Be aware of the difference between assertive and aggressive approaches. People do respect courage and strength and an assertive response gives a clear message. "I can and will defend myself. I am strong".

You may consider saying something like this:

"Sonny, I have asked to talk to you because there is something we need to clear up. I have been getting annoyed a lot lately, even angry. You may not have realised this and you may be just mucking around, but I'm not sure. The first thing I want to say to you is that I don't want trouble, I don't want to fight, I don't want you in trouble and I am hoping we can sort things out before things get any worse. All I want is to be treated fairly and left alone. We used to get on fine, I don't know what happened. I hope we can sort things out but if we can't I'm going to have to take things further. I wanted the chance to talk with you first. Do you have a problem with me?"

Another method of helping people, particularly boys, has been to teach them some of the material I gleaned from the 'Rock and Water'[1] course I completed some years ago. The purpose of this course is to teach self-control and help develop self-confidence. Activities are built around simple self-defence exercises that teach the importance of retaining balance and defending yourself. These have been extremely empowering. The emphasis is about control and balance of the body as well as the mind.

"Chinese Boxing" is a game teaching self-control. It is a quick, engaging game played by two people standing about a metre apart. They extend their hands out in front, shoulder height, palms facing forward, and position their feet about shoulder-width apart. The game revolves around a series of hand taps or pushes, with each player trying to knock the other off balance.

There are two primary strategies to score points. The first is by attacking with just enough force to push the opponent backward, causing them to lose balance. The second strategy is a bit trickier, as it involves using the opponent's strength against them: by dodging or deflecting a push, you can make the other person overextend, leading them to stumble forward. A point is scored each time a player manages to cause their opponent to move one foot. With a quick game to five points, it's a fun, short competition that's great for practicing balance and focus.

This is very useful, particularly in dealing with people who are prone to losing their temper. The skill of retaining balance is improved as a person learns how to attack and defend by taking the impact in their knees like the suspension on a car. Locked knees make it harder to retain balance. A student should be encouraged to find and keep their 'centre'. This is the point of balance in both attacking and defending. As I usually take the role of the opposition, I explain the activity and seek permission to engage in it with them. This activity

---

[1] - Rock and Water. Freerk Ykema. The Men and Boys Program. The Family Action Centre The University of Newcastle, Callaghan NSW 2308.

is not as much about winning as it is about balance and self-control. The spirit of competition adds to the fun.

The most powerful aspect of this game is in drawing a parallel between the importance of physical balance and control, with that of mental and emotional balance and control.

- If a bully can get you to feel weak, the bully has won a point
- If a bully can get you upset, the bully has won a point
- If a bully can get you to surrender power, the bully has won a point
- If a bully can get you angry to the point of lashing out, the bully has won the point.

On the other hand

- If a bully can't make you feel weak, you have won the point
- If a bully can't get you upset, you have won the point
- If a bully can't get you to surrender power, you have won the point
- If the bully can't make you angry to the point of trouble, you have won the point.

You will learn to stay balanced and in control of yourself. We cannot control the actions of others but must control and be responsible for our own. This activity can be repeated over a period of time if a person is responsive and is benefiting from it. I often remind boys that to be a man you need to be in control. Self-control is the beginning of power. I sometimes keep a score chart on my wall or get the individual to keep a record of points won and lost over a week as an incentive. I may even offer a little reward from time to time.

Simple blocking exercises have also proven helpful in empowering boys in particular. Most boys when wanting to start a fight do so by pushing the other in the chest or shoulder. It appears they are trying to provoke the person they are pushing into throwing the first punch.

This is getting a little away from the bullying topic, but its value is not so much in the exercise as it is in the confidence it builds. This confidence has proven very useful in helping boys recover, making them safe, stronger and more importantly, to feel safe.

There are four simple moves to learn in this blocking exercise. Explain that you are going to push them four times. With each push, they learn and apply a different response.

Push 1

Two people face each other about 1 metre apart. One is the person doing the pushing, the other is the recipient.

- The person being pushed is to stand strong and balanced, feet slightly apart.

- The person being pushed it to make strong eye contact with the pusher.

- The person doing the pushing pushes (with permission) the other on the shoulder.

- The person being pushed is to stand strong, resisting the push.

- Encourage the recipient to be stronger, applying more strength and resistance.

- Repeat this until you as the pusher can feel the strong, necessary resistance.

- The pusher should be able to feel their strength and resistance.

- When you feel their strength, offer praise, saying "That's strong, good job."

Positive reinforcement encourages them to try harder. If the person feels weak when pushed, it gives the pusher a sense of power. But if the person pushing feels resistance and strength, it sends the message back that - I am strong.

Push 2

The first four steps of Push 1 are repeated. After the pusher feels the strength and resistance, they say "tough guy" and push again (the second push).

This time, the receiver twists sideways, moving the shoulder being pushed backward to avoid contact, causing the pusher to stumble slightly forward. The receiver maintains balance and eye contact, without moving their feet.

Many people tend to turn their head with their shoulder and lose eye contact. It's important to work on overcoming this habit. Practice on both sides of the body and encourage the person to stay alert and pay attention to the attacker's preferred hand.

Push 3 The block.

With the third push, the receiver blocks the push by bringing their arm, clenched into a fist, up on the inside of their forearm forcing it outward, beyond their shoulders. They should hold it there with strength.

This move should be practiced slowly at first on both sides of the body.

Once grasped, the hand should move with strength and speed, as if suddenly released from a tensioned spring.

After completing the block, the receiver's hand should remain in a strong position.

This same technique can also be used to block a punch. It's important to maintain balance and eye contact throughout the move.

Push 4 Disarming move

On the fourth push, the receiver disarms the attacker by combining steps two and three.

This time, when the shoulder is twisted, the blocking arm grabs the pusher's wrist, pulling them forward and off balance.

This is the only move where the receiver moves their feet.

As the receiver twists, they grab the wrist, pull the pusher through and take a step back with one foot while turning sideways.

The grabbed wrist is held firmly and lifted up and the receiver pushes down with their other arm on the pusher's shoulder blade, holding them in a powerless position.

Maintaining balance is crucial in this move.

These exercises can be practiced weekly and they can be encouraged to practice the moves with a trusted friend. Most people I have tried this with have loved it.

Points to Remember:

- **Start with balance and control.** Both physical and mental balance are crucial for staying in control
- **Avoid pacing.** Pacing often happens when someone is nervous, and it disrupts balance and focus
- **Stand strong.** Keep your head up, big shoulders, and maintain strong eye contact
- **Breathe slowly and deeply.** When under threat, people often breathe quickly and shallowly, depriving the brain of oxygen. Deep breathing helps keep your mind clear and focused. Use self-talk - "I can handle this"

- **Stand still with feet shoulder-width apart.** Keep your knees slightly bent to absorb any impact

- **Maintain a safe distance.** Stand about two metres away from the attacker, out of reach of any sudden movements. This distance gives you time to respond. The attacker's forward movement can help use their momentum against them. Keep your head up and maintain eye contact to avoid surrendering power

- **Keep things equal.** If you're sitting when approached, stand up. A person standing over you holds the power, but standing puts you on equal terms

- **Don't ask "Why are you doing this?" or "What have I done?"** These questions surrender power and control. Stay strong and confident.

It is not my intention to encourage people to fight, but rather to teach them to stand strong and protect their power when faced with bullying. The true value of these exercises lies in building confidence and resilience. I cannot overstate how empowering these practices can be. Some people, motivated by the sense of self-control and strength they gain from these exercises, have even pursued self-defence as a serious interest. The real power doesn't come from physical confrontation, but from the belief and understanding that they can handle situations, empowering them to face challenges with confidence.

Peer mediation is another powerful tool for schools, particularly when it comes to resolving conflicts. I firmly believe that it's always better to teach and empower people to confront and solve problems themselves, when they are capable. Support them, but involve them in the process. This approach is what education and life are truly about.

Mediation is ideal for resolving conflicts, where the individuals involved are generally of equal power. However, when it comes to bullying, the power imbalance is often significant and, in these situations, the focus should shift toward more restorative safer methods, such as **Shared Responsibility.** While mediation allows students to work through differences collaboratively, bullying requires a different approach, one that helps restore balance, ensures accountability and protects the victim being traumatised any further.

"Becoming bully proof"

Ava was a shy and nervous Year 8 student, struggling with a lack of confidence. She found it difficult to navigate social situations and often didn't know how to connect with her peers or gain acceptance. Her limited social skills made it challenging for her to fit in. As a result, she often felt isolated or unsure of herself.

Over the years, I grew close to Ava and came to understand her better. Because of her quiet and nervous nature, Ava often found herself the target of bullying. Her body language was shy and she presented herself as timid and vulnerable, which unfortunately made her an easy target. However, what I admired most about Ava was her determination to overcome her struggles. She was always eager to learn and improve, seeking ways to stand on her own two feet. She was open to building her confidence and self-esteem, and although she faced many challenges, she never gave up. With every rough time, Ava grew stronger, developing new skills and gaining more confidence. When she first joined our school, she was near the bottom on the popularity ladder.

In Year 10, Ava faced her greatest challenge in overcoming bullying. She had a small but supportive group of friends and things seemed to be going well when she started dating a boy. This new relationship caught the attention of a group of three girls who made it their mission to bring Ava down. They constantly bombarded her with embarrassing and invasive questions about her relationship and personal life, pushing her into a humiliating spotlight. Their questions focused on sexual activities and experimentation, setting her up as a target for ridicule and laughter from the entire class. Thankfully, this group was in only one of her classes, but that did little to make the situation easier. The class quickly became an unpleasant and hostile environment for Ava. She struggled to deflect or respond to the cruel comments and rumours spreading about her. As the bullying escalated, Ava found it harder to control her emotions and began expressing her distress openly. The situation grew unbearable and she reached a point where she felt like she couldn't face it alone.

Ava continued to work with me, developing her assertiveness and building her confidence. However, as the bullying intensified, she realised that she couldn't handle this situation. Despite her strong desire to resolve it on her own, she found herself at a loss for what to do. Ava knew about my work with overcoming bullying, particularly the **Shared Responsibility** program and in a moment of desperation, she agreed to let me assist and speak with the girls involved.

Before taking any action, I made sure she fully understood the process, explaining what I planned to do. Once we proceeded, the outcome was immediate and successful. The bullying stopped and Ava was not targeted again.

I share this story not just to highlight the effectiveness of the Shared Responsibility method, but to show how a person, with the right support, can develop the skills and confidence to become "bully-proof" and begin to reach their true potential. I reminded Ava that by empowering us to assist her she had in fact, taken strong assertive action herself in responding to and overcoming her bullying problem. If someone breaks into your house you don't have a problem going to the police. If someone is causing us distress, we don't always have to face the challenge alone. Sometimes seeking support is an important part of growth. I continued to work with Ava, supporting her as she navigated her journey of personal growth and self-discovery.

By the time Ava reached Year 12 she had completely transformed. She had risen to become School Captain, served as a House Captain and represented the student body on the School Council. Ava was also an active member of 'Youth Parliament' and involved herself in various causes and extracurricular activities. She was flying high. Her confidence, skills and assertiveness had grown so much that she could stand in front of the entire school and lead assemblies with ease.

When it came to bullying, Ava proudly declared, "I am now bully-proof!" She had worked hard to build herself up and was now focused on achieving her full potential, no matter what that might be. Through her journey, she gained the respect of her peers and finally understood what it truly meant to be 'popular.'

Looking back on her experiences, Ava confidently stated, "If someone tried to bully me now, it wouldn't bother me at all." Her days of being bullied were behind her and she was living proof of the power of resilience and personal growth.

To effectively combat bullying, individuals can develop and practice key skills that foster resilience and empowerment.

Summary of skills used for Overcoming Bullying
1. **Self-Control:**
2. **Perseverance - Resilience**
3. **Assertiveness:**
4. **Mediation:** Understanding mediation and restorative practices in relation to bullying.
5. **Self-Defence:** The value of self-defences in building confidence and self-esteem.
6. **Self-Belief**

CHAPTER THIRTEEN

RESTORING HOPE

Responding to bullying in Schools.
To the Parent: Embracing Restorative Approaches in Dealing with Bullying

"What is your child facing at school?"

What is your child experiencing at school?

Our schools have fought long and hard over the years to find better ways to respond to and manage bullying. Despite the effort, the challenge remains ever-present. In this chapter, I want to share a story that may offer you a glimpse into what it's really like for your child at school. It's a story that aims to challenge a common misconception: the belief that uncovering facts and searching for the truth is always the most effective way to combat bullying.

Many schools still rely on what I call, "The Detective Method," when responding to bullying incidents. This is a method that involves gathering evidence, interviewing witnesses and trying to pinpoint the truth that lies behind a bullying incident. Research has shown that while this method is well-intentioned, it often misses the mark in addressing the deeper emotional and psychological impact bullying has on a person.

The process involves:

- investigating
- interviewing witnesses

- taking statements
- gathering evidence
- searching for and finding the truth
- punishing.

Many schools continue to rely on this investigative approach, even though it has produced little or no evidence of its effectiveness. It is time-consuming and, at times, potentially harmful to the person who has been bullied.

This process of investigating bullying incidents is lengthy and, unfortunately, rarely produces the concrete evidence needed to resolve the issue.

Research into what schools do to combat bullying has uncovered the following challenges:

- **Witnesses often prove unreliable** – they either didn't see anything or provide conflicting accounts that complicate the situation
- **Statements often contradict each other** with some even shifting blame back onto the victim
- **Friends will lie to protect friends** complicating efforts to uncover the truth
- **Accused students frequently become defensive** and uncooperative, making it difficult to gather useful information or find a solution
- **Evidence is hard to uncover**, particularly when the victim is socially isolated or already unpopular, making their claims seem less credible
- **Students are often hesitant to speak up** due to fear of becoming targets themselves or being labelled as a "dobber" (informant).

The reality is, in pursuing these investigative methods, schools run the risk of adding even more stress and pressure to an already traumatised student. The focus on uncovering the truth or gathering evidence often unintentionally exacerbates the victim's emotional burden. Even if it were possible to identify the perpetrator and collect enough evidence to prove bullying has occurred, this approach still fails to address the root of the issue or offer a solution to the underlying bullying problem.

A true story.

A caring teacher noticed that Luca was likely being bullied. She had observed a group of boys in the class mocking him and it was clear that Luca wasn't coping well with their taunts. Over time, Luca began to isolate himself, choosing to sit alone and withdrawing from his classmates. Concerned, the teacher kept him after class one day to ask if everything was okay. Initially, Luca insisted that he was fine, but when it came time to leave, he hesitated, his fear becoming apparent. The teacher noticed a group of boys waiting outside the door and gently asked if he was worried about them. At that point, Luca broke down in tears. The teacher quickly noted the names of the boys in the group and escalated the matter to the year-level coordinator. Luca and the boys were called out of class and the coordinator asked if there was a problem. Luca remained silent and the group of boys denied any wrongdoing, insisting that everything was fine. Unfortunately, instead of resolving the issue, the situation worsened. The bullying intensified and soon Luca started avoiding school.

A few weeks later, the coordinator reached out to Luca's parents to follow up on his recent absences. Luca's mother expressed concern, explaining that her son had been very ill and unwilling to attend school. She had taken him to the doctor, but the doctor confirmed that there were no physical issues.

In light of this, a meeting was scheduled to discuss the situation further. A few days later Luca, his mother and the coordinator met at the school. After some hesitation, Luca reluctantly admitted that he felt unsafe in his class. The coordinator assured him that the matter would be looked into, but emphasised that the top priority was getting Luca back into school. By the end of the meeting, Luca agreed to return the next day.

At recess, Luca found himself cornered by a group of aggressive boys who were actively trying to provoke a fight between him and one of their members. A teacher on yard duty noticed the escalating tension and intervened, escorting the group - including Luca - straight to the coordinator's office.

Luca, still shaken, tried to muster up the courage to tell the coordinator privately about the incident. However, the coordinator, opting for a more direct approach, gathered all the boys together and declared that he was determined to get to the bottom of the situation and put a stop to it.

The boys were then instructed to sit in different areas of the corridor and write statements about what had transpired. Luca knew that the odds were stacked against him. He was painfully aware that the others would stick together and that his account would likely be dismissed in favour of theirs. In that moment, he felt isolated and hopeless. No one seemed to care. It seemed as though no one was willing to listen to his side of the story or believe him. He even felt abandoned by his mother for making him return to school and, in his mind, he was alone in this battle. No one understood, no one was on his side and there was nothing he could do to change it.

The coordinator dedicated a significant amount of time reviewing the statements, trying to piece together what had actually occurred. The most convincing evidence pointed to a strong belief among the students that Luca had been the instigator and was therefore to blame for the incident. To gain further insight, the coordinator spoke with a few reliable and trusted students from the class, hoping they could provide more clarity. Unfortunately, they either couldn't offer any new information or chose not to get involved. One student did confirm that she had seen Luca with the group during recess and it appeared that he was looking for a fight.

The coordinator also conducted individual interviews with the boys in the group. By this point, the students had become defensive and visibly upset. They denied any wrongdoing and were resentful of being blamed for something they insisted wasn't their fault. Each of them stuck to their version of events, asserting that Luca had started the altercation. They repeatedly referred to their friends for support, relying on their peers to back up their stories.

The coordinator called Luca into his office once more. With a stern and authoritative tone, he confronted him about the group's version of the events. He informed Luca that, after reviewing the evidence and speaking with the other students involved, as well as others from the class, it appeared that Luca had not been entirely truthful in his account of what had happened. Luca, visibly upset, attempted to explain the ongoing bullying he had been experiencing. He wanted to share the details of what had been happening to him, but the coordinator quickly interrupted him. He stated firmly that Luca could not simply accuse others without providing concrete evidence to back up his claims.

"He stood alone as a victim, he now stands alone as one accused of lying, or as one in need of providing proof to substantiate his suffering and pain."

"Maybe you should try being a bit friendlier Luca."

"There are more constructive ways to deal with your frustrations than resorting to fighting."

"Try to lighten up a bit, don't take everything so seriously."

Deep down, I want to believe that the coordinator knew that Luca was the true victim, but his investigation couldn't provide the hard evidence needed to substantiate this. Faced with the complexities of the situation, it was easier for him to take the safe, neutral approach. In the end, the coordinator decided to issue a three-day suspension to two boys involved in the "near fight" - Luca was one of them. The other boys were given stern warnings that any further involvement in similar incidents would result in their own suspension. This, however, was nothing more than a verbal deterrent. No official records or lasting consequences were made beyond the paperwork required for the suspensions.

After the suspension, Luca became the target of even more relentless bullying. The entire class branded him a "dobber" and the torment only escalated. He was accused of getting Brian in trouble and causing his suspension. As a result, Luca was ostracised, never again accepted as part of the class. The bullying continued and Luca suffered in silence, isolated from his peers. His concerned teacher continued to check in with him, offering support: "If you'd like, Luca, I can speak to the coordinator about what's going on and see if we can find a way to help." But Luca always refused, begging the teacher not to say anything to anyone. A few months later, Luca's parents decided to move him to a different school. At that point, the problem just simply and conveniently disappeared.

Let's take a moment to consider the school's objectives and methods in responding to this problem.

I believe the school genuinely intended to:

- **Address the issue as effectively and efficiently as possible**
- **Resolve the problem by initiating an investigation**
- **Gather statements from everyone involved in an effort to understand the situation**
- **Encourage the cooperation of all students involved**
- **Uncover the truth by finding and analysing the story**
- **Interview witnesses in an attempt to verify and support statements**
- **Evaluate the evidence to determine who was at fault**

- **Impose appropriate punishment, discipline and consequences to hold the guilty students accountable**
- **Resolve the problem to a satisfactory conclusion, bringing it to an end.**

These intentions are all well-meaning, but the method used by the school must be critically examined in light of the outcomes. Let's take a closer look at what happened:

- **The investigation was time-consuming and unproductive**
  Despite the school's best efforts, the investigation did not yield any meaningful results or lead to an acceptable resolution

- **The taking of statements complicated the matter**
  The process of gathering statements added pressure on the victim, forcing him to substantiate his experience. Instead of feeling supported, the victim began to feel alienated, even perceiving the coordinator as unsympathetic

- **Efforts to uncover the truth were frustrating and unfruitful**
  The truth, which might have been crucial to addressing the bullying, remained elusive. In attempting to dig deeper, the investigation only exposed the complexities and contradictions within the students' accounts

- **Witnesses were unhelpful and sometimes added confusion**
  Witnesses failed to clarify the situation and, in some cases, their accounts only served to muddy the already complicated issue

- **The bullying students became defensive and uncooperative**
  Rather than reflecting on their actions, the bullies became entrenched in their own defence, refusing to acknowledge any wrongdoing

- **The bullying students were not held accountable**
  Despite the school's efforts, the bullies faced no real consequences and no evidence suggested that the behaviour would stop. This left the issue of bullying unaddressed

- **The problem remained unresolved and the bullying continued unchallenged**
  As a result of the investigation's failure, the bullying persisted and the method proved unable to stop the harmful behaviour

- **The process left the victim more vulnerable than before**
  Rather than offering a solution or assisting the victim, the school's actions left him feeling more helpless and isolated, increasing his distress rather than alleviating it

- **The victim became the accused and was punished**
  Through a flawed process, the victim ended up being suspended, reinforcing his sense of victimisation and further alienating him from the school community. The school thought it was fair and right to administer equal consequences

- **The victim ultimately left the school**
  The culmination of these failures prompted the victim's family's decision to take him out of the school, highlighting the complete lack of support and resolution.

If the school had been asked at the beginning of this process what outcomes they were hoping to achieve, it's certain that none of the above would have been included in their goals. The intentions were likely to stop the bullying, support the victim and ensure a safe and respectful environment for all students. Unfortunately, the method used, despite being well-intentioned, resulted in outcomes that not only failed to resolve the issue but, in some ways, worsened the situation for Luca.

Luca's story is not an uncommon one. Even if Luca had said or done something that initially contributed to the situation, and there is no evidence to suggest he did, that doesn't justify or excuse bullying in any form. His suffering was both severe and relentless and he faced overwhelming numbers and power stacked against him. Bullying is fundamentally about power - the abuse of it - and the school should have been able to recognise this dynamic and respond in a way that addressed the real issue: the imbalance of power and the harm it was causing to Luca.

Research has revealed that this punitive approach to handling bullying is largely ineffective and unfortunately all too common. Schools often treat bullying incidents in the same way they might address conflicts, behavioural issues, or peer group tensions. Bullying is fundamentally different and requires a tailored, more selective approach. Simply applying the same methods used for other issues fails to address the deeper issues at play, particularly the imbalance of power and the emotional toll on the victim.

Research has shown that the R**estorative Approach** in dealing with bullying has proven to be far more effective in changing the behaviour of bullies and providing genuine support to victims. Unlike traditional fact-finding or punitive methods, this approach focuses on getting to the heart of the matter: the suffering and distress experienced by the victim. My first book, ***Shared Responsibility: Beating Bullying in Australian Schools***, presents and outlines a restorative method that has proven to be very successful.

I must emphasise that this restorative method is distinct from mediation or traditional restorative practices. While both approaches have their merits, they often place victims in a vulnerable position by having them go face-to-face with their tormentors - sometimes even outnumbered. If a victim possesses the confidence and resilience to engage in a face-to-face meeting, I fully endorse it. However, from my research, experimentation and hands on experience, I have seen the harm that can arise from putting the victim in the same room with the tormentors. Having learned and recognised the complex power dynamics at play in bullying, my research does not endorse face-to-face meetings with the bullies and their victims together.

In the story above, this school failed in several critical ways:

- It did not identify and respond to bullying effectively
- It did not provide a safe environment for the student
- It neglected its duty of care toward all students.

This assessment may sound serious and harsh, but bullying itself is serious and harsh. Luca was not only a victim of his tormentors; he also became a victim of his own school's procedures.

The "Detective Method" of responding to bullying can lead to several unintended, damaging outcomes:

- It places teachers or staff members in the difficult role of acting as policeman, prosecutor, lawyer, judge and jury simultaneously
- It often leaves the accused feeling defensive, resentful, unfairly treated and even more determined to retaliate
- It can lead to intensified bullying, with aggressors targeting victims with even greater hostility
- It risks driving bullying behaviours underground, making them harder to detect and manage

- It often leaves the victim feeling more isolated and vulnerable than before
- It creates an environment where bullying can continue unchecked and even thrive.

A message to schools.

Streamline your efforts and skip the witnesses, statements and excessive interviews. Listen to victims' stories with openness and empathy, setting aside judgment. What's most important is not what has happened, but what will happen next. Stay neutral and focused on solutions, not facts. "The most important consideration is that one of your students is experiencing distress and feels unsafe."

Channel your energy into empowering students to contribute to solutions and actively support victims. Finding "the truth" or getting the full story does little to stop bullying. The truth that matters is this: some students in your school may be suffering in silence and in need of immediate support. The central focus in responding to bullying should be the wellbeing of the victim, ensuring they feel heard, supported and safe. Schools should continually evaluate and refine their approach to bullying, always asking: are these methods effective? Fact-finding often results in blame and punishment, while **Shared Responsibility** fosters collaboration to build and sustain a safe, supportive environment for every student.

Shared Responsibility is about assisting students to feel and be safe. If you're interested in a restorative approach with proven success in combating bullying, consider exploring **Shared Responsibility** – *Beating Bullying in Australian Schools*. This resource is available in both hardcover and e-book formats, providing an effective, structured method for schools working towards a supportive, safe environment for all students.

If you're a parent working with your school on a bullying issue, ask direct questions about their policy, procedures and processes. Are they investigative and punitive, or are they restorative? Don't get caught up in policy language - focus on understanding the actions that bring the policy to life. It's essential to learn what steps they actually take, rather than getting lost in promotional jargon.

CHAPTER FOURTEEN

FAMILY SUPPORT

Supporting Your Child Through Bullying

"Be wise and careful in the advice you give your children."

Things are never straightforward when dealing with bullying issues. There are often many variables, expectations, ideas and imposed solutions to contend with.

One complication that can cause some concern is the 'well-meaning parent'. This is the parent who gets involved and tries to solve the problem without having the expertise or knowledge to do so.

From my experience the most common advice the 'well-meaning parent' gives their child, is to fight back. "If anyone gives you a hard time, I give you permission to bash them."

This advice is rarely followed as most children who are bullied fear the bully and what the parent is asking them to do is not within their power. This well-meaning advice can inadvertently add to the stress of an already struggling individual. Instead of helping, it has the potential to cause additional trauma, fear and isolation. This person is likely already dealing with feelings of embarrassment and shame from being bullied and the pressure to meet the parent's expectations only intensifies these emotions. As a result, the person often feels even more isolated, unable to share their struggles with their parents, as they fear disappointing them.

Louis was constantly teased and tormented by Kai, who was known as the toughest kid in the class. Kai surrounded himself with a group of friends and he went to great lengths to impress them. During sports, Kai would deliberately throw balls at Louis with all his strength, taking every opportunity to bump into him or knock him to the ground. In games like basketball and hockey, Kai found ways to assert his dominance and hurt Louis. He would shove him into the goalpost or intentionally strike him in the shins with a hockey stick, as if these actions were part of his weekly routine. Whenever Louis was within reach, Kai would strike, making every moment an opportunity to assert power.

Louis was struggling with what to do. Kai was big and strong, while Louis was small. Physically, Kai embodied everything Louis aspired to be. He feared that if he reported the bullying, things would only get worse, so he stayed silent. One day, when Louis's dad noticed bruises on his arms, he joked about the need to keep his guard up and fight back. Over time, however, his dad sensed that something deeper was going on. It wasn't just harmless horseplay.

Louis was relieved to finally talk about it. *"Dad will know what to do; I'm not alone anymore."* He explained everything: the punching, the bumping, the bullying in sports. He showed his dad bruises he had been hiding. His dad's expression turned serious. *"What do you do when he hits you, son?"* Louis didn't answer. He just stared at the kitchen floor, feeling small and helpless. His dad's tone shifted to anger, *"I'll tell you what you do. The next time he lays a hand on you, turn around and plant one right between his eyes, as hard as you can. That'll make him think twice about touching you again. I don't care what the school says, you have a right to defend yourself."*

There was nothing that Louis would like to do more, but he knew it was only a dream. He had never been in a fight in his life. Kai was scary and there was no way he could take him on, let alone beat him in a fight. Louis didn't want to show his fear or tell his dad he couldn't do it. He wanted his dad to be proud of him. Louis admired his dad. He possessed all the toughness and courage that he longed for. Every few days his dad would ask, *"Have you fixed that kid up yet?"* Louis kept his bruises covered and lied to avoid disappointing his dad. Louis thought, "I don't want dad to hate me, to be angry with me or think I'm weak."

This "well-meaning" dad, despite his good intentions, did nothing to help his son. Instead of offering support or seeking a solution, he only pushed Louis's pain deeper inside him. By encouraging Louis to fight back, he inadvertently increased his son's anxiety, making him feel more alone and misunderstood. Rather than helping Louis confront the bullying in a healthy way, his advice left him with no real strategy to cope, just a sense of pressure and fear.

A young person being bullied needs support but what is advised and/or expected must be within their capabilities. Most young people want to be able to look after themselves and solve their own problems. Being bullied often comes with feelings of helplessness, weakness, failure and self-hatred. The 'well-meaning' parent tries to empower and protect their child by teaching them that violence is the answer. In reality, violence hasn't solved many problems at all. Even if a child does muster enough courage to hit back, the parent is teaching the child to deal with the problems in a very unhealthy way.

The 'well-meaning' parent often creates confusion for the child by contradicting the school rules. Schools cannot condone violence. What does a child think or learn when the school is issuing consequences for something that their parent told them to do? Parents can cause further confusion for their bullied child when the child fights back and hits a sibling at home and is punished for it. What values do we teach our children when there are obvious contradictions?

The problem can be further complicated when a parent receives notification that their bullied child is being suspended for fighting. The parent often tries to justify the action as retaliation and accuses the school of failing in their duty and not doing anything about the bullying problem in the first place. The question is, did the school know anything about the bullying problem in the first place? The parents of a bullied student have a right to be angry and expect a safe and supportive school environment for their child. However, the parents and the school need to work together to ensure this is provided, not only for their own child, but for all students. Giving advice that contradicts the school's policies and procedures will not achieve this goal. Schools are required by law to have policies and procedures in place and parents need to display confidence in the school when dealing with such issues. If the school fails to deliver then there are avenues to pursue.

There are many 'well-meaning' parental statements that complicate bullying issues and make things more difficult for schools to manage.

> "Whatever they do to you, do it back to them, only harder."
> "If they bother you, hit first and ask questions later."
> "Find something they don't like and pick on them."
> "Go get your brother, he'll fix them."
> "Take Joel with you, he doesn't tolerate any nonsense."
> "Tell them if they don't watch out, I'll come to school and they can deal with me."

This last statement raises a further complication. It occurs when the 'well-meaning' parent tries to solve the problem by personally approaching the accused bully or contacting their parents. They don't stop long enough to realise that an aggressive threat against another person constitutes bullying itself. Such a deed could even result in legal action. A response of this type more often than not complicates the problem and the school can be suddenly faced with a number of angry parents all demanding action on an issue that the school previously had little or no knowledge of.

Most parents are naturally defensive of their children and when contacted by the 'well-meaning' parent of a 'professing victim', could be excused for feeling the need to rise up and protect their child, or at least ensure that the facts are correct. If parents are going to take this approach, they need to carefully choose their words if a positive, cooperative outcome is hoped for. It is far better to let the school deal with the issue according to policy and procedures. In such a case the victim no longer has to deal only with the bully, the chances are they now have to contend with the bully's parents and family as well. When a bullying child feels the support and backing of their parent, they are less likely to be cooperative with the school.

In responding to one such incident it took quite some time to convince the parents to agree to leave the issue with the school. There were threats and reminders from both families. "If the school doesn't fix things quickly then we will take matters into our own hands." Fortunately, all the students involved understood the situation and were cooperative. The school followed their documented procedures and the desired result was achieved. The normal follow-ups took place over three weeks and confirmed an end to the problem. However, such complications can and may impact on the effectiveness of any system given the possible variation in method and beliefs.

Bullying has never been solved by bullying. This type of intervention by parents can only make the situation more complicated and place the victim under further pressure.

The goal is to get all people involved working on the same page, working together towards achieving a common objective. The objective is to help the recipient to be safe, feel safe and to stop the bullying. It has been my experience that getting the parents to work with the school has been more challenging than getting the students to cooperate. Parents usually say, "Well, I will let you give it a try, but believe me, if you don't put an end to it, then I will." Fortunately, the students have been a dream to work with in comparison.

Be wise and careful in the advice you give your children.

One angry parent said to me, after his daughter had been refusing to come to school for a week as a result of bullying, "If this system can fix the problem, then I will personally write to the Principal endorsing the method and strongly recommend that all schools take it up." The girl was back at school in two days and the problem disappeared. I'm not sure if the letter ever arrived.

'Well-meaning' teachers can also cause complications when they bypass the approved school procedures and attempt to deal with bullying issues in their own way. Threats like "If this doesn't stop, I'll …..," are largely ineffective. Detentions and angry outbursts, very rarely produce the desired objectives. Private, unstructured, friendly 'off the record' chats with an accused bully, are often quickly forgotten or not taken seriously. Aggressive intervention often pushes the bullying underground and diminishes any confidence that the recipient may have had in the school to help.

Unfortunately, some of the old-style teachers learnt to teach and survive using bullying tactics and have found it difficult to change. Teachers who tell students to 'toughen up' or 'stop telling tales' or 'don't be a wuss' need to catch up with the modern and legal world.

If you're not satisfied with how the school is handling a bullying situation, consider scheduling a meeting with school leadership to discuss their policies and procedures. Ask if these procedures were followed and whether they are achieving the goal of providing a safe environment for all students. If the results are falling short, it may be an opportunity for the school to revisit and improve its approach to bullying management.

Some parents need to have their quest for justice or revenge satisfied. They find it difficult to accept that the person doing the wrong thing gets off free, that is, without punishment. I can understand this. My **Shared Responsibility** method acknowledges that people do learn from consequences and it allows the freedom for the school to impose consequences if and when it feels appropriate. However, I do not advise this, as I believe premature consequences have the potential to reduce the effectiveness of the method. When a student is punished without being given an opportunity to learn and put things right, the entire psychology of the system is changed. The bullying student needs to take responsibility for their actions, assist and be empowered to fix the problem. When they do, they take a big step in growing up and learning some valuable lessons about life and themselves.

CONCLUSION

THE POWER WITHIN

Throughout this book, we've explored the many layers of bullying and its impact on both the emotions and the mind. This book has provided strategies designed to help anyone who has been bullied discover and reclaim their power. The strategies shared here, building assertiveness, utilising humour, developing strong body language, using drama and even selective ignoring, are not mere theories. They have emerged from years of study, research, experimentation, counselling and real-life stories of people who have faced and overcome bullying in its many forms. Their stories have been shared to help others find inspiration, strength and courage from within.

Each chapter shows that empowerment is not about changing who we are, but about embracing resilience, confidence and self-worth. For some, that might mean practicing a strong stance, standing tall and confident even in difficult moments. For others, it's discovering the skill of deflecting negativity with humour, or practicing how to remain unphased in the face of hurtful words.

My hope is that every person who reads this book will find their unique path to resilience and, as each of these stories shows, empowerment that begins with small but brave steps.

The journey from feeling powerless to feeling empowered is one of growth and self-discovery. It may involve setbacks and challenges, but the techniques in this book are tools, stepping stones toward standing up to bullying in constructive and resilient ways. The methods described are designed not only to manage the impact of bullying but to build lifelong skills in self-confidence, composure, emotional and mental strength.

My hope is that this book has shown you that although bullying can leave a lasting impact, it does not have to define you. With practice and support, every person can develop skills to stand up, protect their power and move forward with strength and dignity.

My hope is that the stories and strategies shared within these pages inspire and empower young people, parents, students, teachers, youth workers, welfare workers, counsellors, chaplains and all who support young people who face the challenges of bullying. Together, we can make a lasting impact on the lives of those affected by bullying by looking to **The POWER WITHIN.**

Fly high my friends and may you achieve the ultimate goal of becoming bully-proof.

OTHER BOOKS

BY IAN FINDLEY

Shared Responsibility Beating Bullying in Australian Schools

Website: www.ifindbooks.com.au

Email: ifindbooks3@gmail.com

ACKNOWLEDGEMENTS

I would like to extend my heartfelt thanks to the many special people who have inspired, supported, and encouraged me in sharing my knowledge and experiences through this book.

To my longtime friend, Jenice Stokes—thank you for being the spark behind my first book, and once again offering your time, thoughtful feedback, and careful proofreading for this one. It was you who first recognised the strength and impact of the anti-bullying strategies I used and urged me to write them down so they could help others.

To my wonderful wife, Julie—thank you for your constant support and patience throughout the writing and preparation of this book. Your help with typing, your willingness to listen and offer feedback, and your careful proofreading have been invaluable. More than that, you have always stood beside me, encouraging me to pursue my dreams and share what I've learned.

I would also like to acknowledge and thank Deborah Patterson, retired Principal, for reading through the manuscript and offering valuable feedback. Your professional insights and thoughtful comments were much appreciated.

To my daughter, Kristen, an Assistant Principal—thank you for your insights, ideas, and practical recommendations. Your input has been deeply appreciated.

To my son Jared and daughter-in-law Dee—thank you for allowing me to include the picture of my beautiful granddaughter, Harper. Her presence in this book brings a very personal and meaningful touch.

A sincere thank you to Kev, Les, and the entire team at Busybird Publishing. Your guidance, patience, and encouragement throughout the publishing process have made it a pleasure to partner with you on this, my third book with your support.

Finally, I dedicate this book to every individual who has ever found themselves on the receiving end of bullying. This book is for you. What I share within these pages is drawn from real experience—strategies and approaches that have helped many rise above their pain and reclaim their strength. It has been my privilege to walk alongside them on their journey.

www.ingramcontent.com/pod-product-compliance
Lightning Source LLC
Chambersburg PA
CBHW061233070526
44584CB00030B/4100